MEASURING SUCCESS AS JESUS DID

by Randy Southern

Published by Cook Ministry Resources
a division of Cook Communications Ministries

4050 Lee Vance View
Colorado Springs, Colorado 80918

Colorado Springs, CO/Paris, Ontario
www.cookministries.com
Printed in U.S.A.

Author: Randy Southern
Designer: Rebekah Lyon
Editorial Team: Cheryl Crews, Matthew Eckmann, Janna Jones, Gary Wilde, Gayle Wise, Vicki Witte

TABLE OF CONTENTS

WHY DISCIPLESHIP?

Discipleship is a well-worn word. It's been used to justify everything from programs to events. But have you ever wondered what was in the mind of God when He invented the whole concept? His infinite wisdom could have created any method to accomplish His purpose in our lives. But this all-wise God simply told us to "make disciples."

Though there are many definitions for it, we could all agree that discipleship includes the process of learning and following Christ. And the bottom line is to become like Jesus, right? As Christians, we talk a lot about doing and not enough about being (God made us human beings, not human "doings"). He desires us to be conformed to the image of His Son (Romans 8:29). That process begins at salvation and continues until we arrive on heaven's shore.

So why disciple teenagers? Why not another program or "instant growth" gimmick? Why not entertainment or the newest ministry fad? Why discipleship?

First, because students need it. Pick up your newspaper or take a walk through the halls of your local high school if you need motivation. Second, Jesus commanded and modeled it. And third, history confirms it. Put simply, it works. It avoids the prevalent quick-fix, "decision" mentality and focuses instead on a long-term lifestyle. Discipleship is not a program. It's God's plan. It involves sharing with your students both the Word and your life, which leaves a lasting impact (1 Thessalonians 2:7-8).

Discipling teenagers doesn't require that they be good-looking, intelligent, well-balanced or popular (think of the original dozen in Jesus' group!). It only requires students who are faithful learners and willing followers of Christ.

Some might say teenagers aren't ready for discipleship, that they can't handle the meat of the Word or the challenge of following Christ. Theirs is sort of a "junior Christianity." They don't have what it takes to become great for God. But we know better, don't we? So did Joseph, David, Daniel, Shadrach, Meshach, Abednego, Mary, and John Mark.

So does God.

The original Twelve disciples weren't much when they began, but they changed the course of human history. If we only had the first part of their story, we wouldn't hold out much hope for them—knowing their frequent faults and failures. But you know the rest of the story. The same is true for your students. The rest of their story is yet to be written. That's where you come in. This book is actually divided into two parts: Part One is contained in the following pages. But Part Two is yet to be written—and God has given you the opportunity to be part of writing that story as you touch your students' hearts with your life day by day.

This world desperately needs Christian youth to rise up and to answer the call of Christ to "come follow Me." This book will help them do that.

So pour your life into them. Impart the Word to them. Believe in them. Don't give up on them. Disciple them. And most of all,

Enjoy the journey!
Jeff Kinley

WHY CUSTOM DISCIPLESHIP?

So, you're convinced that what your students need is discipleship. So, why *Custom Discipleship*? Because *Custom Discipleship* acknowledges and deals with the two seemingly contradictory but central truths of discipleship.

1. There are Biblical principles that remain constant for all disciples of Jesus.

Custom Discipleship teaches students about the life of Christ and the example He set for Christians. Those stories are unchanging. The truths that Jesus communicated through word and example are the principles by which all Christians can truly live.

2. Discipleship is a dynamic, ever-changing process.

Custom Discipleship provides options that allow you to customize the learning process to meet the needs of the students in your group—no matter where they are in their relationship with Christ. This ability to customize the material keeps it dynamic and relevant to the lives of your students. Each lesson also contains *Learner Links* and *Making it Real* discipleship tips to help small-group leaders learn to share their lives with students and to grow alongside the students they are leading.

Custom Discipleship is a curriculum designed to blend the power of these truths. Let it help you as you take the challenge of discipling youth and obey Christ's command to make disciples.

Jeff Kinley is a veteran student minister, dedicated to students, parents, and youthworkers as a life calling. He is the author of several successful books, including No Turning Back, Never the Same *and* Done Deal, *(David C. Cook Church Resources). A gifted communicator, Jeff is a frequent speaker at conferences and youth camps. Jeff and his wife Beverly, have three sons—Clayton, Stuart and Davis.*

KEY QUESTIONS are the focus of the lesson. Students should be able to answer these by the end of the session.

BIBLE BASE gives the scripture references that are the basis for the whole session.

THE OPENER is optional to the session. It is a great way to get kids involved before diving into the study.

SESSION **3**

WHAT A SERVANT FEELS

Key Questions
- How do our own painful experiences equip us to help others who are hurting?
- What kind of an example did Jesus set when it came to empathizing with people who are hurting?
- How can you empathize with hurting people?

Bible Base
Matthew 25:31-46
John 11:1-44
Romans 12:15

Supplies
- Flip chart
- Pens
- Pencils or pens
- Index cards
- Copies of Resources 3A, 3B, and Journal

Opener (Optional)

Common Ground
Ask your students to pull their chairs into a circle. Choose one of your group members to start the game standing in the middle of the circle. Remove his or her chair from the circle (think Musical Chairs). The person in the middle will call out a category. The category may be anything from "Collects comic books" to "Born in another state" to "Hates country music." Everyone in the group who fits the category must stand up and run to an empty seat. The person in the middle, meanwhile, must also try to get to an open chair. The person who doesn't make it must then stand in the middle and call out the next category.

LEARNER LINK
This Link activity is designed to stretch your students' brains a bit. Many of the answers on Resource 3A may sound very close to correct but are not the best answers. Watch to see how deeply your kids struggle with the issue of suffering. This question has been asked through the centuries, and there is no easy answer.

This activity may prove to be an effective bonding exercise for your group members. They may be surprised to find out that other people in the group share their interests, experiences, or background.

MAKING IT REAL
As you get to know your students better, pray for them specifically. Taking the time to do this will help you to focus on their needs. It will also help you to continually acknowledge and trust that it is God who is making these kids into disciples of Jesus Christ—sometimes even in spite of your efforts!

CUSTOM DISCIPLESHIP **33**

SUPPLIES listed here are those needed for the core lesson. Any supplies for options are listed with that optional activity.

BOLD TYPE signifies "teacher talk"—things to be said directly by the leader of the group.

THERE ARE THREE LINKS that divide each session, taking students through the learning process and into personal application.

LEARNER LINKS are located through the sessions to give the leader extra tips on how to help their students learn the Word of God.

MAKING IT REAL sections are tips on discipleship located throughout the sessions.

After your group members have weighed in on the topic of Jesus' empathy, ask: **Maybe one of the reasons God allows us to experience pain, suffering, loss, and hard times is so that we will be better able to understand what other hurting people are going through and be better prepared to help them? Why or why not?** Let your group members offer their opinions.

Link 3

Empathy 'n' Me
Ask: **Have you ever had someone say to you, "I know just how you're feeling"? If so, how did you feel when you heard those words? Did you believe the person? Why or why not?** These words are especially popular at funerals. Usually the people who use the phrase don't mean any disrespect by it; they just might not know what else to say.

What if the person really did know how you feel—somewhat, at least? What if he or she had gone through a similar experience? Would you be interested in talking to that person? Why?

After a few students have offered their thoughts, say: **Okay, let's reverse the situation. Let's say you run into someone who's hurting or in need of help. Let's say that the person is going through a situation similar to one you went through a year or so ago. Would you be interested in talking to that person?** If some of your group members express reluctance, listen to their reasons for not getting involved. Invite the rest of the group to respond to those reasons.

The resource sheet "What I've Got to Give" (Resource 3B) is designed to help your group members identify the things in their lives that qualify them to be truly empathetic, the situations and circumstances they've experienced that make them experts of sorts in dealing with specific kinds of hurt.

Encourage your students to take this assignment seriously. Emphasize that no one will be asked to share anything on the sheet that he or she is uncomfortable with.

LEARNER LINK
If any of your group members are brave enough to share their responses to Resource 3B, you will need to respect their feelings, as well as their privacy. You may need to ask a few questions to clarify a point or to correct a possible misunderstanding, but try not to pry for more information. Do not put your students in a position where they feel pressure to reveal more than they want to. When your volunteers finish sharing, be quick to affirm them, and encourage the rest of the group to do the same.

After a few minutes, ask if there are any volunteers who would like to share some of the things they wrote down. After the volunteers have shared, discuss as a group the possibility that there are people in this world who can benefit from the negative things that have happened to us.

MAKING IT REAL
A big part of discipleship is encouraging your students to put what they have learned into action. As their leader, you should be constantly looking for teachable moments—times when you are together with the students, outside of your group time, in which you can encourage them to practice what they have been learning. Another great way to do this is to set up service projects or experiential learning times. Session five in this book provides what you need to set up one of these learning experiences.

Before you wrap up this session, throw out a few more questions to the group: **What if you run into someone who's facing a problem you've never encountered? Let's say you've never had any experience with this kind of problem. Can you still offer that person empathy? If so, how?**

34 CUSTOM DISCIPLESHIP

OPTION ICONS are located at the beginning of each link to let you know that there are options for those groups at the end of the session.

RESOURCE PAGES are noted throughout the session. The actual pages are reproducible and can be found at the end of each session.

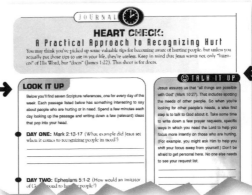

LOOK IT UP! is a section of the student journal page that encourages kids to continue their process of discipleship through the week. It provides a passage of Scripture and a question for each day of the week.

TALK IT UP! provides a place to write down personal prayer requests as well as the needs of accountability partners.

DO IT UP! provides a chance for personal application. It contains a *Plan!* and *Act!* and a *Review!* section to help students put what they learn into practice.

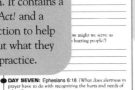

CHECKLIST of options allows you to keep track of which options you have used.

OPTIONS are designed for specific types of groups but provide great variety if you want to mix and match.

EACH ICON represents a type of group and designates options specific for that group.

THIS HEADING tells the section of the session where this option can be used.

NON-PERISHABLE GOODS

Key Questions
- What is the difference between an earthly treasure and a heavenly treasure?
- What did Jesus warn about defining success in terms of earthly treasures?
- How can you invest your valuables in an eternally meaningful way?

Bible Base
Matthew 6:19-21; 7:24-27

Supplies
- Pencils
- Legos
- Copies of Resources 1A, 1B, Journal
- Bibles
- Dominoes

Opener (Optional)

Silent Auction

Bring in items from your home that have some value monetarily, but even more value sentimentally. Display the items around the room where you meet, and include an index card at the base of each item. As the student enter, give them a pencil or pen and have them travel through your displays. A silent auction is conducted when each bidder writes his or her bid on the card before each item displayed. At the end of the time allotted for bids, the highest written bid is accepted.

LEARNER LINK

Be sensitive to the levels of affluence of your students' families. Some students may come from very affluent families, while others may come from families struggling to make ends meet. While making the point of today's session, be careful to neither judge the families of affluent students as shallow and selfish, or over-spiritualize the families that are struggling. Family income is not so much the issue here as how a family chooses to use their income.

As you can guess, the bids from your students might be low, depending on what you have displayed. That's okay. Your goal is to get them to realize that an item with no overt monetary value can be valuable for its memories or what it stands for. At the end of the bidding process (roughly five minutes) collect the cards and have the group members find a seat. As you review the bids out loud, explain why the money bid would never be enough to convince you to part with that item. If possible, tell a brief story about each auction piece and why it is meaningful to you.

MAKING IT REAL

For the next four or five weeks, you will be teaching your students what it means to be disciples of Jesus Christ. One of the most helpful things you can do to help them grow as disciples is to assign "accountability partners." Explain to your group members that, for the next few weeks, accountability partners will be responsible for checking on and encouraging each other's growth as disciples. The partners should plan on hooking up at least twice a week (whether at school or by phone) to update each other on their discipleship efforts.

Ask: **What have you learned about me from this auction? Do any of you have items that may not be worth much money, but are priceless to you? What are they?** (Take responses.)

Explain, **This may have seemed like an odd way to start this lesson, but I wanted to show you that there are two ways to view value. One is with a price tag, the other is with what is inside you. And there is a huge difference between the two.**

Link 1

Building Code

Divide your group into two teams. Give one team a supply of Dominoes and the other team a supply of Legos. When you say, Go, both teams will begin working as quickly as they can to build a tower with the supplies they have. Give the teams a few minutes to build their structures as high as they possibly can. When time is up, you will pretend to judge the structures on their design. As you lean in to examine each building, accidentally nudge the table or desk upon which it's sitting. The Lego structure may wobble a little, but it should remain intact. The Domino structure, on the other hand, will probably tumble like . . . well, like Dominoes.

Discuss: **That's what happens when you try to build something permanent out of something temporary. If you can't tell the difference between the two, you could be in some serious trouble. Have you ever bought or owned something that you thought was permanent or well-built but turned out to be temporary or a piece of junk?** Be prepared to share an example of your own, if you have one. Encourage several students to share their consumer horror stories as well.

Afterward, explain: **In this session, we're going to be talking about how to tell the difference between what is temporary and what is permanent.**

Link 2

Treasure Storage

Hand out copies of "Everything I Ever Wanted" (Resource 1A). Ask your students to get into pairs and work through the questions. (This might be the perfect time to have students pair up with their accountability partners.) Encourage them to be creative, yet realistic, in their responses. After all, there are many different ways for things to be made useless. Give your students a few minutes to work. When they're finished, ask volunteers to share what they came up with.

Next, ask one of your group members to read aloud Matthew 6:19-21. Discuss: **How would you describe in your own words what Jesus is teaching here about possessions? What does it mean to store up treasures on earth?** (It means to use our money to accumulate things that are considered valuable and desirable in our society today.)

What's the problem with accumulating material possessions? (Like the Domino structure in Link 1, material things are temporary. Eventually they will be destroyed, stolen, or ruined—and we will have nothing to show for our hard-earned money.)

What does it mean to store up treasures in heaven? (It means to use our time, energy, and money for things that God considers important and valuable.)

Why are heavenly treasures a much better investment? (For one thing, they can't be destroyed, ruined, or stolen. For another thing, they will retain their value forever.)

Translate Matthew 6:21 into your own words. What was Jesus saying? (Jesus was saying, "The stuff we put our money into shows what we think is really important.")

Do you think this is a fair statement? Why? Maybe another way to say it is, "To find out what is important to someone, look in his or her checkbook." Jesus knew that when He said this He would make people think about their own lives. He knew that one of the quickest ways to assess people's lives is to look at what is important enough for them to spend money on.

Later, Jesus asked people to compare their attitude toward earthly possessions with building a house. Have one of the students read Matthew 7:24-27. Ask, **What did Jesus say we can do to be like the wise man?** Why wasn't his "house" destroyed? But what happened to the foolish builder's house? Why was his house destroyed?

It's obvious that Jesus wasn't talking literally about a building a house, but following His words. Many people do not follow His words, but strive after possessions and earthly treasures. From the two passages we have just read, how does Jesus measure success when it comes to money?

Can you share some examples of people you know (no names!) who seem to equate "success" with "treasures"? Why is it such a temptation to do so? Have you ever been tempted like this?

Link 3

Rock-Solid Investments

Based on what we've studied today about what Jesus said about possessions, would you consider making any changes in your attitude toward money, the way you spend your money, and the things you accumulate? Pass out copies of "If You Got It . . ." Resource 1B. Have students get back together with their accountability partners to answer the questions on the resource. After the pairs are finished with Resource 1B, ask volunteers to share one thing on their list they will do this week to begin to store up treasures in heaven.

As you finish, hand out copies of the student journal, "Heart Check: A Practical Approach to Storing Up Treasures in Heaven" (Resource 1C). Have each student look at the "Do It Up" section and fill out the plan for what they will do this week to store up treasures in heaven.

LEARNER LINK

It will be helpful for each one of your students to have a discipleship notebook. You can create these using three-ring binders or simple file folders. (If your folders are the standard 8.5 x 11 you will need to copy the resource pages at 120%.) Encourage your students to keep all of the resource pages that they receive in this notebook. This will be especially helpful as they work through the daily readings and questions for the "Heart Check" pages. You may also want to provide some extra paper for them to use as journal pages. The whole purpose of this is to help your students see discipleship as an ongoing process and to help them continue to grow outside of the group.

Reassemble the group in a large circle, take out a dollar bill and tell everyone that they will each have ten seconds to hold the bill before passing it on. During that ten seconds they should quickly say something about what first step they are going to take to follow Jesus a little more closely when it comes to their "treasures."

As you conclude the session, point out that the rest of the "Heart Check" student sheet is designed to motivate each group member to set aside a few minutes each day to spend with God. Encourage them to use the sheet as they study God's Word and follow through on their "action plans" to store up treasures in heaven.

MAKING IT R E A L

Encourage your students to share prayer requests with each other. You may want to have a specific time to do this as a group or encourage accountability partners to do it sometime during the week. Ask students to commit to praying for those requests. Encourage your students to include requests related to this session, including asking God to help group members remove the obstacles in their lives that prevent them from storing up treasures in heaven.

Everything I Ever Wanted

Listed below are some "dream possessions," things that can be purchased for the right price. If there are some possessions that have been left out—things that you would probably invest in, if you had the money—add them to the list. Then go through the list and describe how each thing might be ruined or eventually become worthless. Put some thought into your answers. Be creative.

Season tickets for your favorite sports team

An enormous CD collection

A state-of-the-art home theater system

A designer wardrobe

A country club membership

A yacht

A top-of-the-line luxury car

A ten-bedroom mansion

A beachfront vacation home

A motorcycle

Expensive jewelry

A collection of valuable art

Spending cash

IF YOU GOT IT . . .

Over here, make a list of the earthly treasures you have.

_____
_____
_____
_____
_____
_____
_____
_____
_____
_____
_____
_____
_____
_____
_____
_____
_____
_____
_____
_____
_____
_____
_____
_____

Now, list how your earthly treasures can be used for God's work.

_____
_____
_____
_____
_____
_____
_____
_____
_____
_____
_____
_____
_____
_____
_____
_____
_____
_____
_____
_____
_____
_____
_____
_____

HEART CHECK:
A Practical Approach to Storing Up Treasures in Heaven

You may think you've picked up some valuable tips for using your money wisely, but unless you actually put those tips to use in your life, they're useless. Remember, God wants not only "listeners" of His Word, but "doers" (James 1:22). This sheet is for doers.

LOOK IT UP

Below you'll find seven Scripture references, one for every day of the week. Each passage listed below has something interesting to say about the Lord's view of money. Spend a few minutes each day looking up the passage and writing down a few (relevant) ideas that pop into your head.

DAY ONE: Mark 6:6-13 (How would you feel if Jesus gave you the same instructions He gave His traveling disciples?) _____
_____
_____
_____

DAY TWO: 1 Timothy 6:10 (What kinds of evil can be brought on by the love of money?) _____
_____
_____
_____
_____

DAY THREE: Ecclesiastes 10:19 (Do you believe the tone of this verse is serious or sarcastic? Why?) _____
_____
_____
_____
_____

DAY FOUR: Luke 20:20-25 (How would you describe Jesus' attitude toward money?)
_____
_____
_____
_____

☺ TALK IT UP

Jesus assures us that "all things are possible with God" (Mark 10:27). That includes storing up treasures in heaven. So when you're faced with an obstacle that's interfering with your God-honoring spending habits, a wise first step is to talk to Him about it. Take some time to write down a few prayer requests, specific ways in which you need the Lord to guide your financial outlook. (For example, you might ask Him to remind you of what is temporary and what is eternal.) Don't be afraid to get personal here. No one else needs to see your request list.

_____
_____
_____
_____
_____
_____
_____
_____
_____
_____
_____
_____
_____
_____
_____
_____
_____
_____
_____
_____
_____
_____

DAY FIVE: Luke 6:20-23 (Why do you suppose Jesus singled out the poor right at the beginning of this sermon?)

_____

_____

_____

_____

DAY SIX: Matthew 6:24 (How do people serve money?)

_____

_____

_____

_____

DAY SEVEN: Matthew 19:23-24 (What does this tell you about wealth?)

_____

_____

_____

_____

DO IT UP

If you're serious about storing up treasures in heaven, you'll need an action plan. Here is one to follow:

STEP ONE: Plan!

What will you sacrifice this week in order to use your material possessions for eternal things? Put some thought into your response. Be specific. How much money are you talking about? What will you do with it? How will you decide the best way to use it? How can you use a material possession to tell others about Jesus or show His love?

STEP TWO: Act!

Put your plan into action, then answer these questions. Did things work out as you had planned? Was making the sacrifice easier or harder than you expected? How do you feel about it now?

STEP THREE: Review!

Do you think Jesus appreciates your use of your material possessions? Do you feel any different about your money now? Do you think you might make this a regular habit? Why or why not?

LITTLE BIBLE BACKGROUND

Link 2

Give your students a quick true-false quiz to see how much they know about what the Bible says concerning money. Here are the questions:

- **True or false: According to the Bible, money is the root of all evil.** (False. 1 Tim. 6:10 says the love of money is a root of all kinds of evil.)
- **True or false: According to the Bible, having wealth is a sin.** (False. Wealth itself is neither good nor evil. It's what you do with it that counts.)
- **True or false: According to the Bible, rich people are more likely to get into heaven than poor people.** (False. That's what the disciples believed, though. Jesus explained in Matthew 19:24 that rich people can actually have a harder time accepting salvation than poor people—probably because of their dependence on their money.)

Link 3

Ask your pastor or one of your church financial people to talk to your students briefly about the tithes and offerings that are collected every Sunday. Ask that person to explain where the money that is collected goes and how it is used to carry out God's work in the church, in the community, and in the world.

ADVANCED LEARNERS

Link 2

If you'd like to explore the topic of money in Scripture a little further, have someone read aloud Luke 9:1-6. Use the following questions to guide your discussion of the passage:

- **Why do you suppose Jesus sent His disciples out without any money or supplies?**
- **Do you believe there are still disciples in the world who depend on the Lord's day-to-day provisions for their ministry?**
- **Would you ever consider supporting someone like that with your resources? Why or why not?**

Link 3

Get your students' "expert" opinions on the topic of tithing. Use the following questions plus Genesis 14:17-20; Leviticus 27:30; Numbers 18:21; and Malachi 3:8-10 to guide your discussion:

- **What is a tithe?**
- **How seriously should a Christian take the idea of tithing?**
- **How does tithing help us in our relationship with God?**
- **Do you believe Christians owe God anything, as far as their money is concerned? If so, what do we owe Him? If not, why not?**

MOSTLY GUYS

Link 1

To kick off your discussion, do a quick exercise to help your guys see where their money goes. Use the following questions to guide the activity. Encourage your guys to respond honestly.
- **Where does the money you spend come from?**
- **Do you have any monthly bills that you're responsible for—car payments, phone bills, credit card debt?**
- **After you've paid your bills, how much do you have left?**
- **How much of that do you put away for your future?**
- **How much do you spend on your girlfriend, whether it's money for dates, flowers, gifts, or anything else?**
- **How much do you spend on yourself—on clothes, CDs, entertainment, fast food, and anything else you buy?**
- **At the end of the month, what do you have to show for all your hard work, or for your parents' hard work?**

Link 2

To get your guys thinking about the ultimately worthless nature of material possessions, use this line of questioning:
- **What's the dumbest purchase you've ever made in your life?**
- **What made the purchase so dumb?**
- **What made you buy it in the first place?**
- **How did you feel about it after you got it home?**
- **What did you learn from the experience?**

MOSTLY GIRLS

Link 1

Needed: play money

Hand out $500 of play money to each group member and announce that you're taking them on a shopping spree to the mall. Rather than physically traveling to the mall, however, your girls will journey there through their imaginations. Explain: **You have five minutes to spend your money or you lose it. Where would you go and what would you buy?** One at a time, have your girls tell the group how they would spend their $500.
After everyone has shared, ask: **Of the things that you would buy today, how many of them do you think you would still have, use, or wear a year from now?** Let your group members tell you themselves how temporary their purchases would be.

Link 2

Ask an elderly woman from your church to talk briefly to your girls about what it was like to live through the stock market crash and the Depression. If possible, find someone whose family lost almost everything they had. Let your visitor remind your group members just how risky it is to put your faith in money.

MEDIA
Link 1
Needed: video clip

Bring in a video of *Arthur*, a movie that depicts a person enjoying the benefits of great wealth. Play the scene in which Arthur distractedly buys thousands of dollars worth of clothes that he doesn't even want. (Perhaps the best way to find the scene is to fast-forward approximately 30 minutes from the start of the movie.) As you're watching the video, ask your group members to think about how much money they would like to have eventually and how they would like to spend it.

Link 3
Needed: CD or cassette and player

While your group members are working on Resource 1B, play the song "If I Had $1,000,000" by Barenaked Ladies (from the *Gordon* album). The song is a humorous description of things the band members would buy if they had the money mentioned in the title. Ask your group members to suggest some things they would do if they had that kind of money. Then talk about what they do with the money they have now.

EXTRA ADRENALINE
Link 2
Needed: bumper sticker, paper, markers, scissors, tape

Bring in one of the popular bumper stickers for parents of college-age students. The bumper sticker reads, "My son/daughter and my money go to _____ University." Hand out supplies including paper, markers, scissors, tape, and anything else you have handy. Let your students design their own bumper stickers that inform the world where their money goes (or doesn't go). Ask them to consider the principles of Ecclesiastes 2:4-11 and Matthew 6:19-21 as they create their designs.

Link 3
Needed: play money

Hand each student 20 or more dollars of play money. Ask the students to get with their accountability partners and come up with a plan to take this money and help people. After each pair has decided on a plan, have them act out this plan, without using words, so the other members of the group can guess what it is. As you finish, hand out copies of the student sheet, "Heart Check: A Practical Approach to Storing Up Treasures in Heaven" (Resource 1C). Have each student look at the "Do It Up" section and fill out the plan for what they will do this week to store up treasures in heaven.

Link 1

Rather than using the building contest to introduce the idea of temporary structures, ask your group members to participate in a retelling of the story of the Three Little Pigs. If you need some help recalling the story, you'll probably be able to find it in a children's book at the library. As you read or tell the tale, four of your group members should act it out, playing the roles of the pigs and the Big Bad Wolf. Afterward, discuss the story with these questions: **Which of the three pigs got the most for his home investment? Why? What is the safest thing we can invest in?**

Link 2

Needed: Wheel of Fortune™ game board or video clip

If you can get your hands on a Wheel of Fortune board game, bring it in. If not, tape a segment of the TV game show to show to your students. Make sure that the snippet you record includes at least one player landing on "Bankrupt" and losing all of his or her money. Either play a round of the board game or play the clip from the show until someone goes bankrupt. Discuss: **Can bankruptcy happen that fast in real life? Is it possible to lose everything you own in one day?** Get your students talking about how temporary fortune is.

Planning Checklist

LINK 1: Building Code
- ❏ Mostly Guys
- ❏ Mostly Girls
- ❏ Media
- ❏ Junior High

LINK 2: Treasure Storage
- ❏ Little Bible Background
- ❏ Advanced Learners
- ❏ Mostly Guys
- ❏ Mostly Girls
- ❏ Extra Adrenaline
- ❏ Junior High

LINK 3: Rock-Solid Investments
- ❏ Little Bible Background
- ❏ Advanced Learners
- ❏ Media
- ❏ Extra Adrenaline

PERFECT PRIORITIES!

Key Questions
- What do your actions and decisions say about your priorities?
- How can misplaced priorities damage your soul—and thwart success as Jesus taught it?
- How can you make sure your soul is protected when your priorities influence important life decisions?

Bible Base
Matthew 16:24-27

Supplies
- Pencils
- Copies of Resources 2A, 2B, Journal
- Gumball machine, full of gumballs
- Pennies, three per student
- Bibles
- Variety of keys

Opener (Optional)

Quote-Unquote
Hand out copies of "Say What?" (Resource 2A). Give your group members a few minutes to complete the sheet. When they're finished, ask volunteers to share which quotes they understand and which ones they agree with. Ask students why they agree and disagree with the ones they do.

Discuss: **Which of these sayings, if any, come from the Bible?** (Three of them come from God's Word: "If anyone wants to be first, he must be the very last" (Mark 9:35); "Faith is being sure of what we hope for and certain of what we do not see" (Heb. 11:1); and "What good will it be for a man if he gains the whole world, yet forfeits his soul?" (Matt. 16:26). A fourth, "Actions speak louder than words," is based loosely on James 2:14-17.

LEARNER LINK

This opener may seem a little random, but the discussion is to help you illustrate for your students how important it is to know God's Word. Sometimes, phrases from the Bible become so overused as cliches that we are not sure what they mean anymore. Remind the students that its important to learn the Bible for themselves, instead of just reducing it to bumper-sticker slogans.

How would you explain these quotes to a non-Christian friend in a way he or she can understand? Let your students take turns trying to simplify the words.

Explain: **Later in this session we're going to talk some more about one of these quotes, and we're going to find out what a difference it can make in our lives.**

MAKING IT REAL

Introduce your group members to the art of journaling. Ask your students to keep a journal or diary of their observations, feelings, and frustrations as they take steps each day to be a more devoted disciple of Jesus Christ. Encourage them to be consistent in writing in their journals. Point out that journaling may be difficult at first, but that the more they do it, the better they will become. Furthermore, the better they become, the more they will benefit from it.

It's All about the Lincolns

If you handed out Resource 1C at the end of Session 1, take a few minutes at the beginning of today's meeting to find out how well your students did at reexamining what is truly valuable in their lives. Ask volunteers to share their experiences, both positive and negative, with the rest of the group. Encourage other group members to offer their generous praise and helpful criticism. Your group members should feel comfortable enough with each other to be completely open and honest about struggles and successes.

This opening activity will require a little preparation on your part, but the effort will be worth it. First, you'll need a selection of keys—everything from house keys to luggage keys to old-fashioned gate keys. The more shapes and sizes of keys you can find, the better. Next, you'll need a stack of pennies—three for each group member, to be exact. Finally, you'll need a child's gumball dispenser—the kind that requires pennies—filled with gumballs. (These are fairly inexpensive at most toy stores.) Display the keys and pennies prominently for your group to see. Keep the gumball machine hidden, though, until the end.

Explain: **I've got some tasty treats waiting for the first person who can unlock the container they're in. You may have noticed the keys and the pennies on display. Your job is to find the one that will open the container. I will give you each three pennies. Each key will cost you one cent. If you use your money wisely and make the correct choice, the treat will be yours.** It's important that you read these instructions word for word, if possible. They are truthful, but designed to be misinterpreted.

Let your students "buy" the keys one at a time. Each person will get to choose one key, then wait for everyone else to pick before choosing the second key, and so on. It's important that you collect the pennies students "spend," so that when the buying is done you have all the pennies.

With your students holding their keys, tell them that the prize is a supply of gumballs. Show the gumball machine and announce that all it takes to access the prize are the pennies you gave your students.

When they protest about being misled, explain it this way: **I never told you that you had to spend all your pennies to buy keys, but that seemed to be what you wanted to do. How does it feel to know that you gave up something you needed to get something you didn't?** Get responses from a few of your students. **This very idea of choosing your priorities—like deciding to sacrifice something valuable to get something that's ultimately worthless—is the topic of our session today.**

To introduce the subject of priorities, ask your group members to name their dream jobs—the careers they would choose if looks, size, education, training, or qualifications didn't matter. Most likely your group members will name things like actor, model, athlete, entrepreneur, and so on. Use these questions to make your students think a little deeper about what they'd give in order to reach their career goals:

• **What things would you be willing to give up in order to become a professional athlete?**
• **Would you be willing to sacrifice your health by playing when you're hurt and enduring injuries that might affect you later in life?**
• **Would you be willing to give up your time by devoting 12 to 15 hours a day to training, practicing, and things like that?**
• **Would you be willing to put personal relationships on hold because of all the demands of travel and fame?**

• **Would you be willing to let go of your own privacy when fans start following you and asking for your autograph everywhere you go?** Let students suggest any other priorities that would need to be examined. Pause after each question to allow time for responses.

Use the same line of questioning for any career your students name, making specific changes where necessary. For example, if someone names acting as a dream job, you might ask: **Would you be willing to give up your personal appearance if you were told you needed plastic surgery?** If students choose more practical careers, ask if they would be willing to sacrifice the time and money necessary for the education and training required.

Your goal is to find out how far your students would be willing to go in order to make their career dreams come true. Where would they draw the line in the sacrifices they would be willing to make? Periodically ask students to explain why they would be willing to make certain sacrifices and whether they think those sacrifices might one day come back to haunt them.

Introduce the Bible study portion of the session with this simple question: **What do you suppose Jesus has to say about what we should or shouldn't sacrifice in order to keep our life priorities the way we want them?**

Link 2

Everything but the Soul

Ask one of your group members to read aloud Matthew 16:24-27. When he or she is finished, ask someone else to read verse 26 again. Discuss: **What kind of person was Jesus talking about in this verse?** (At first glance, He seems to be talking about greedy, power-hungry people willing to "sell their souls" to get ahead. In reality, though, the verse could be about anyone who allows his or her priorities to get out of balance.)

What is this *soul* that we're talking about? If no one else mentions it, suggest that our soul includes our intimate relationship with the Lord. It is the eternal part of us that will either live forever with Jesus or suffer eternally apart from Him.

In human terms, how valuable is your soul? (Your soul is the most valuable part of you. It is more valuable than anything else in the world.)

What do you think it means to "forfeit" your soul? If no one else mentions it, suggest that it means to trade your relationship with Jesus for something else. But instead of gain, you end up losing the most important thing.

Besides money and possessions, what are some other things that many people prioritize that might cause someone to forfeit his or her soul? (Popularity [or fame] is a motivating factor for many people. Some would be willing to do—or give up—just about anything to be popular or famous. The desire for love, security, or stability might also cause a person to take desperate measures, as far as his or her soul is concerned. Some people are willing to sacrifice everything for the approval and acceptance of others.)

Do you think it's possible for a person to forfeit his or her soul and not even realize it? (If a person's priorities are such that he or she is pursuing things other than what Jesus wants us to pursue, it could be quite easy to ignore the soul and eventually forfeit it without even noticing.)

Give some examples of specific situations in which a person may be tempted to forfeit his or her soul for the sake of something temporary. Let your group members offer a few ideas.

What would you say is the basic difference between the priorities of the world and the priorities of Jesus? (The world tells us to satisfy our own needs, to spend our time doing whatever it takes to get things that will make us "happy"—in a shallow, temporary way. Jesus tells us to deny ourselves, to take up His cause—His mission for our life—and follow Him, letting Him reward us in ways that will make us happy for eternity.)

Link 3

Counting the Cost

Let's look at some examples. Hand out copies of "No Small Sacrifice" (Resource 2B). Let your students work in pairs to complete the sheet. When they're finished, go through the questions as a group. Use the following questions to guide your discussion.

What are your choices in this situation? What would you have to gain? What would you have to lose? If you were really facing a situation like this, what would you do? Why? How would your life's priorities influence your decision? Encourage several group members to respond honestly.

Next, hand out copies of Resource 2C "Heart Check: A Practical Approach to Perfecting Your Priorities.Have students work with their accountability partners to look at the "Do It Up" section and fill out the plan for what they will do this week to keep their priorities in line with the teaching and example of Jesus—and thus protect their soul—when they make decisions. The sheet is intended to motivate each group member to weigh the long-term effects of a decision against the short-term gains. If some accountability pairs finish before others, encourage them to share things that they can pray about for each other during the week.

LEARNER LINK

If you have students who join your group and do not have accountability partners, you may want to discuss the questions with them. As soon as you have two new students, pair them up as partners. You may also run into times when students are absent. When that happens, work with the number of students you have: pair students without partners together or be the partner for an extra student yourself.

As you conclude the session, point out that the rest of the "Heart Check" student sheet is designed to motivate each group member to set aside a few minutes each day to spend with God. Encourage them to use the sheet as they study God's Word and follow through on their "action plans."

MAKING IT REAL

Some of your students may have needs that don't get addressed during your group time. Make a special effort to get to know all of your students individually. That may mean a phone call or a trip to a sporting event or a lunch together. Not only will this help you build relationships with the students, but their seeing you outside of your discipleship group will help them connect what they learn to their everyday lives.

When your students are finished making their plans, make one last point: True discipleship involves following Christ and doing His will, wherever that path may lead. If you strive to follow Jesus with all your decisions, your priorities should reflect His as well.

Say What?

Below you'll find a list of several well-known sayings. Circle the ones you understand. Put a star next to the ones you agree with.

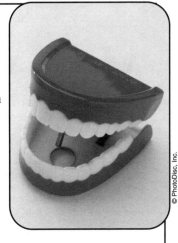

If anyone wants to be first, he must be the very last.

Actions speak louder than words.

Faith is being sure of what we hope for and certain of what we do not see.

A friend in need is a friend indeed.

All you need is love.

All's well that ends well.

What good will it be for a man if he gains the whole world, yet forfeits his soul?

Sticks and stones may break my bones, but words will never hurt me.

Beauty is only skin deep.

God helps those who help themselves.

No Small Sacrifice

1) Health Professional (conscience clause)
2) Gay Lifestyle (workshop)

Each of the following scenarios requires a prioritizing decision—and perhaps a sacrifice—on your part. Read each one and then answer the questions that follow.

The Promotion

The manager of the local video store tells you how much he appreciates the excitement and enthusiasm you bring to your job. In fact, he appreciates you so much that he's promoting you—to assistant manager! Not only will this promotion double your hourly pay rate, it will also allow you to work more hours each week. He asks if you would be available to work after hours Friday night. "We're adding an adult section to the store," he explains, "and I need someone to help me rearrange the shelves to block that section off from the rest of the store."

You love your job at the video store. You know the customers. You know which films to recommend to which people. You're good at what you do. The people you work with are your friends. With TV screens mounted on the ceiling, you get to watch movies while you work. On top of all that, with your pay rate doubled and your hours increased, you should be able to put away some serious cash for college.

In fact, things would be perfect if it weren't for the new addition to the store. The idea of renting porno movies makes you nervous. You know what your parents would say about it, but then they never come into the store, so you wouldn't have to worry about them finding out. Same thing with your youth group leader and your friends from church. The only person you really have to worry about is yourself.

© PhotoDisc, Inc.

What are your choices in this situation?

What would you have to gain by keeping your job? What would you have to lose?

What would you have to gain by finding another job? What would you have to lose?

How would your life's priorities influence your decision?

The Test

Your best friend calls you Monday evening after missing school that day. You remind her about the history test she missed that morning. "Duh," she replies. "Why do you think I faked being sick today? I didn't have a chance to study this weekend, so I had to do it today. If I don't pass this test, I won't pass history. And if I don't pass history, my mom won't let me go to church camp this summer. But the good news is that Mr. Peters is going to let me take the test tomorrow."

"Did you study?" you ask.

"Not yet," she replies. "I knew there was no way I could get through six chapters in one day, so I thought I'd wait until I find out what I need to know."

That's when it clicks in your brain: she wants you to tell her what was on the test! When you start to protest, she cuts you off. "It's not like we're cheating. I'm not asking you for the answers; I'm just asking for the questions. I'll study what I need to know, but why waste my time studying things I won't need?"

If it were anybody else in school, you would have hung up by now. But this is your best friend—the girl who helped you fix your bike when it was broken, the girl who makes church camp fun, the girl who's always been there when you've needed her. This is the first time she's ever asked you to do anything like this for her.

Unfortunately, although your friend doesn't believe that what she's asking is cheating, Mr. Peters would probably disagree. And while it may not be cheating, you know it's not right.

What are your choices in this situation?

What would you have to gain by doing what your friend asked? What would you have to lose?

What would you have to gain by refusing to tell her what was on the test? What would you have to lose?

How would your life's priorities influence your decision?

HEART CHECK:
A Practical Approach to Perfecting Your Priorities

You may think you've picked up some valuable tips for making wise decisions at today's meeting, but unless you actually put them to use in your life, these tips are worthless. Remember, God wants not only "listeners" of His Word, but "doers" (James 1:22). This sheet is for doers.

LOOK IT UP

Below you'll find seven Scripture references, one for every day of the week. Each passage listed below has something interesting to say about matching your priorities to Jesus'. Spend a few minutes each day looking up the passage and writing down a few (relevant) thoughts that pop into your head.

DAY ONE: Deuteronomy 30:16 (What are some incentives for making choices that honor the Lord rather than ourselves?)

_____

_____

_____

DAY TWO: Proverbs 10:2 (What is the problem with "ill-gotten treasures"?)

_____

_____

_____

_____

DAY THREE: Matthew 4:8-11 (What did Jesus say when Satan offered Him the entire world?)

_____

_____

_____

DAY FOUR: Philippians 1:9-11 (How can we discern what is best for us?)

_____

_____

_____

☺ TALK IT UP

Jesus tells us that "all things are possible with God" (Mark 10:27). That includes following Jesus by maintaining the right priorities when you make everyday decisions. So when you're faced with a really difficult situation, like going against what you believe in order to help a friend, a wise first step is to consult the One who makes all things possible. Take some time to write down a few prayer requests, specific ways in which you need the Lord to help you keep your priorities in line and make smart choices. (For example, you might ask Him to help you weigh the long-term effects of a decision against the short-term gains.) Don't be afraid to get personal here. No one else needs to see your prayer request list.

_____

_____

_____

_____

_____

_____

_____

_____

_____

_____

_____

_____

_____

_____

DAY FIVE: Psalm 119:30 (What does it mean to choose the way of truth?)

_____

_____

_____

_____

_____

DAY SIX: 1 Corinthians 4:4-5 (What kind of decisions do you think the Lord will praise?)

_____

_____

_____

_____

DAY SEVEN: Proverbs 10:9 (What is integrity? What are some dangers of taking crooked paths?)

_____

_____

_____

_____

DO IT UP

If you're serious about making God-honoring priorities and choices, you'll need a plan of action. Here is one to follow:

STEP ONE: Plan!

What are you going to do this week to live by Jesus' priorities when you make decisions? Put some thought into your response. Be specific. What exactly are you planning to do? At what point in your decision-making process will you do it? How will you change the way you make decisions?

STEP TWO: Act!

Put your plan into action and then answer these questions. Did things work out as you had planned? Did your plan make your decision-making easier or harder? Have you noticed any difference in the decisions you made?

STEP THREE: Review!

Do you think you're doing enough to protect your soul in other areas of your life? Is there anything more you can do? If so, what?

LITTLE BIBLE BACKGROUND
Link 2

If your students have trouble understanding what happens when you forfeit your soul, bring up the topic of reputation. Ask: **What would you think of your best friend if he got drunk one night, beat up his girlfriend, threatened to kill himself, and ended up in jail? Would your opinion of him change? If so, how? Let's say he came to you a few days later, apologizing and saying he didn't know what had made him snap. Do you think you'd ever be able to look at him in the same way again? Would his reputation ever be the same again? How long do you think you'd remember what he did on that one night?** Point out that those same principles hold true for Christians who forfeit the soul's values for ultimately worthless things. We may think forfeiting our soul's values is a temporary thing, that we can make it up later. But more damage is done than we can imagine—damage to our Christian reputation and damage to our witness.

Link 3

Hand out copies of Resource 2B. Ask your students if anything like this has ever happened to them. Ask them to identify the problem areas and the moral decisions implied in both stocking pornography and a friend asking for answers. You might need to refer them to specific portions of Scripture that relate to both these areas (e.g. lust: Matthew 5:27-28; honesty: Exodus 20.) Ask for a couple of volunteers to act out their responses once they have written out some answers.

ADVANCED LEARNERS
Link 2

Here's a question that should stir up some debate among students who are familiar with Christian teachings: **How many times can a Christian compromise the priorities of his or her soul before permanent damage is done?** Some students may suggest that each time we make a decision that goes against our Christian beliefs we weaken our relationship with the Lord a little more. Others may counter that God's forgiveness assures us that no matter how many times we make poor decisions, He will restore us to fellowship with Him if we admit and are truly sorry for what we've done.

Link 3

After you've gone through the examples on Resource 2B, ask your group members to examine another situation—this time, one from real life. Using the same questions you used on Resource 2B, help your students look at a specific situation one of them faced in which there was an opportunity for temporary gain, but only by sacrificing Christian priorities.

MOSTLY GUYS
Link 1

If you've got a group of all guys, add a few more questions to your discussion of "willing sacrifices":
• **How much would you be willing to sacrifice to date the hottest girl in school?**
• **Would you be willing to give up the girl you're interested in now?**
• **Would you be willing to sacrifice your reputation if your new date was known for being a little "loose"?**
• **Would you be willing to sacrifice your sexual standards?**
• **Would you be willing to sacrifice your friends in order to hang out with her friends?**

- Would you be willing to give up your beliefs about the importance of taking care of your body if you found out that she was a smoker, a drinker, and a pothead?
- What has happened to your priorities? Where was the line that you were willing to cross?

Link 3
Substitute "The Test" scenario on Resource 2B with the following situation:
Total Recall
You're hanging out in the locker room after practice with four other guys when your best friend turns to you and asks, "What were those jokes we heard on the radio this morning?"

That morning you rode to school with your friend, who, as usual, was listening to Howard Stern, and who, as usual, was laughing his head off. Meanwhile, you were wondering how anyone could get away with saying the things that were being said on the air.

Now your best friend can't remember the jokes and is asking you to repeat them. You would love to be able to make the other guys laugh, but you're uncomfortable with repeating the things you heard.

If you say you can't remember the jokes, you'd be lying. You remember all of them. If you claim the jokes weren't that funny, the other guys will still want to hear them. If you refuse, they'll want to know why.

What are your choices in this situation?
What would you have to gain by telling the jokes? What would you have to lose?
What would you have to gain by refusing to tell them? What would you have to lose?

MOSTLY GIRLS
Link 1
If you've got a group of all girls, add a few more questions to your discussion of "willing sacrifices" in Step 1:
- How much would you be willing to sacrifice to become part of the best clique in school?
- Would you be willing to sacrifice the friends you have now?
- Would you be willing to start gossiping and making fun of others in order to fit in?
- Would you be willing to sacrifice your reputation as someone who's nice to everyone?
- Would you be willing to sacrifice your beliefs about smoking and drinking?
- Would you be willing to sacrifice your sexual standards in order to do what everyone else in the group is doing?
- What has happened to your priorities? Where was the line that you were willing to cross?

Link 3
Replace "The Promotion" scenario on Resource 2B with the following situation:
The Invitation
Your boyfriend invites you to spend the night in a hotel room he has booked for prom night. Most of the other couples you're going to prom with are doing the same thing. Your boyfriend promises that things won't get sexual.

"Prom night is the biggest night of our high school lives!" he explains. "I just want to spend it all with you and not have to worry about getting you home by a certain time."

To do what he's asking, though, you will have to tell your parents that you're spending the night with a friend. Your friend, of course, has already told her parents that she's spending the night with you.

What are your choices in this situation?
What would you have to gain by going along with your boyfriend's plan? What would you have to lose?
What would you have to gain by refusing to go along with the plan? What would you have to lose?

MEDIA

Link 1

Needed: video: *The Gift of the Magi*

Bring in a video of *The Gift of the Magi*. Show a few clips (be sure to screen the clips ahead of time) to your group members to give them an idea of what the story is about. Include the scenes in which the characters sacrifice their most valuable possessions in order to buy something for each other, only to find out that their gifts were made useless by their sacrifices. After showing the clip, ask: **Can you think of any other situations in which sacrificing something in order to get something else turned out to be a bad decision?**

Link 3

Needed: Steven Curtis Chapman's "For the Sake of The Call" and CD player

After you have discussed your students' answers to Resource 2B, play the song, "For the Sake of the Call." Talk about the priorities that are represented in the lyrics and some of the difficulties that the students face if they organize their priorities as Jesus did.

EXTRA ADRENALINE

Link 1

Needed: pennies, bowl

Add some extra action to this activity. Rather than having your students buy keys with their pennies, let them try to toss their coins into a large bowl (similar to the kind of games you might find at a fair or carnival). Mark off a line about seven feet from the bowl for group members to stand and throw pennies. To introduce the game, say something like this: **I'm going to give each of you three pennies. You see the line on the floor and the bowl in the middle of the room. The only other thing you need to know is that there is a prize for the winner.** With that, step up to the line and toss a penny at the bowl.

Your students will take turns throwing their pennies at the bowl. Some of the coins may land in the bowl; most will not. It doesn't matter. After all of the pennies have been thrown, collect them from in and around the bowl. Make sure you get them all.

Announce: **The winner is the first person who can bring me one of the pennies I gave you.**

When your students protest about being misled, explain it this way: **I never told you to throw your money toward the bowl, but I figured you knew what you were doing. How does it feel to know that you sacrificed something important for nothing?**

Link 3

Rather than simply discussing the scenarios on Resource 2B, ask a couple of your group members to act them out. Your volunteers should perform each scenario twice, the first time depicting what might happen if the person went along with the plan and the second time depicting what might happen if the person refused. Encourage your actors to play the scenes as realistically as possible.

JUNIOR HIGH

Link 1

Use this scenario to begin your discussion: **Let's say your dad gives you one of his old baseball cards as a present for your birthday and tells you that you can do anything you want with it. His only request is that you not sell it. He believes that baseball cards were meant to be traded, not sold. According to**

the collector's guide, the card is worth over $2,000. **What would you be willing to trade it for?**
Encourage your students to be as specific as possible. For example, if someone says he'd be willing to trade the card for a car, ask: **What kind of car? Would you trade it for a used Camaro? What if it was over 20 years old? What if it had a little rust on it?** Your goal is to find the minimum your students would be willing to give up the card for.

Link 3
Substitute "The Promotion" scenario on Resource 2B with the following situation:
The Request
The two best players on your soccer team are skipping practice to go to a concert. You know that because they told you. They also told you to tell the coach that they're on a field trip for school.
This is important, you see, because the coach has a strict rule about missing practice. Unless you have a very good excuse, if you miss the practice before a game you're not allowed to play in the game.
It just so happens that tomorrow's game is the first round of the league tournament. Your team, the number one seed, is playing the worst team in the league. Without your two best players, though, there's a good chance you'll lose the game and your season will be over. If, however, you go along with your teammates and they're allowed to play, there's a good chance your team will win the tournament and advance to the regionals.
At practice, the coach asks you if you know where the two missing players are.
What are your choices in this situation?
What would you have to gain by going along with your teammates' plan? What would you have to lose?
What would you have to gain by refusing to go along with their plan? What would you have to lose?

Planning Checklist
LINK 1: It's All about the Lincolns
❑ Mostly Guys
❑ Mostly Girls
❑ Media
❑ Extra Adrenaline
❑ Junior High

LINK 2: Everything but the Soul
❑ Little Bible Background
❑ Advanced Learners

LINK 3: Counting the Cost
❑ Little Bible Background
❑ Advanced Learners
❑ Mostly Guys
❑ Mostly Girls
❑ Media
❑ Extra Adrenaline
❑ Junior High

3

DOWNWARD MOBILITY

Key Questions
- What does it mean for a Christian to "get ahead" in life?
- What example did Jesus set with the people He spent time with and the way He treated them?
- How can you follow Jesus' example by learning to value the privilege of being last?

Bible Base
Matthew 4:23-25
Mark 9:33-35
Luke 19:1-9
John 4:4-42

Supplies
- Bibles
- Pencils
- Copies of Resources 3A, 3B, Journal

Opener (Optional)

The Mark 9:35 Pentathlon

Kick off your meeting with an unusual five-event competition. Explain that none of the events require athletic skill, so everyone has an equal chance of winning. Below you'll find five suggestions for events. Feel free, however, to substitute your own ideas, using the supplies you have on hand. Also, adjust these suggestions for the size of your group and the space of your meeting room.

- *Paper Basketball*—Students get five chances to shoot a paper wad into a trash can from ten feet away.
- *Toilet Paper Roll Bowl*—Students get two tries to knock down as many toilet paper rolls (set up like bowling pins) as possible by rolling a tennis ball.
- *Marble Finesse*—Students get five chances to roll a marble into a taped-off circle (approximately two feet in diameter) from about ten feet away.
- *Ping-Pong Paddle Flip*—Students will see how many consecutive times they can keep a ping-pong ball in the air by hitting it with a paddle, alternating sides of the paddle after each hit.
- *Dice Roll*—Students get five rolls to total the highest score.

The scoring for each event will be based on the number of competitors you have. If there are six people in your group, first place will be worth 600 points, second place will be worth 500 points, and so on, down to last place, which will be worth 100 points. You will keep track of the scores.

What your students won't know, though—and won't find out until after the fourth event—is that the goal of

LEARNER LINK

It probably won't surprise you that your students will want to win. There is something about competition that brings out the worst—and sometimes the best—in all of us. Jesus knew that people view life as a competition. Reflect this opener back to the first session about priorities. It is important that your students see the links between each lesson and the theme of "success" as described by Jesus. Ask them what their attitude toward competition reflects about their priorities.

MAKING IT REAL

As you get to know your students better, pray for them specifically. Taking the time to do this will help you to focus on their needs. It will also help you to continually acknowledge and trust that it is God who is making these students into disciples of Jesus Christ—sometimes even in spite of your efforts!

the competition is to finish with the fewest number of points. Just before you begin the fifth and final competition, announce who's leading overall. Your students will probably be shocked to hear that it's the person they assumed was in last place.

If anyone grumbles or questions your scorekeeping, say: **Oh, didn't I tell you that in this competition the first will be last, and vice versa? Your goal was to score as few points as possible!**

Armed with this knowledge, your students may try to "throw" the last event, in order to score the fewest points. However, that will be difficult to do, since the last competition is the dice roll. They will be at the mercy of the numbers that come up.

Ask your winner: **How did it feel to have the fewest points and be announced the winner?** Ask your student with the most points: **How did it feel to think you were ahead, only to find that you had lost the game?**

Link 1

The Joy of Being Last

If you handed out Resource 2C at the end of Session 2, take a few minutes at the beginning of this meeting to find out how well your students did at setting priorities in the decisions they made. Ask volunteers to share their experiences, both positive and negative, with the rest of the group. Encourage other group members to comment on the volunteers' experiences.

To play this variation of the "Hot Potato" game all you'll need is a kitchen timer and a potato (or anything else small that your students can pass quickly). Have your group members sit in a circle. When you start the timer, students should pass the potato to the left. When the timer goes off, check to see who is holding the potato. In the normal game, that person would be out. In this game, however, you will award 100 points to the person on his or her right—the last person to touch the potato before the timer went off. The winner is the one with the most points after a designated number of rounds. When your students figure out how to win the points, they will become very creative in their strategies to hold the potato until the last moment!

When the game is over, ask: **Can you think of any other games or situations in which it pays to be last?** Let students offer any ideas they come up with. **In today's session, we're going to talk about some radical advice from Jesus encouraging us to strive for last place.**

Link 2

V. 35 If anyone wants to be first, he must last and the servant of all.

Do What?

Ask one of your group members to read aloud Mark 9:33-35. Discuss: **What do you think Jesus meant by this? What does it mean to be "the very last" or "the servant of all"? What kind of attitude does it take? How is it shown in your actions?** (From an attitude standpoint, it means not thinking of ourselves as being better than anyone else. From an action standpoint, it means putting the needs of other people—especially those who are considered underprivileged—ahead of our own. Encourage students to be specific.)

How did Jesus practice what He preached? Get a few responses from your group members.

Matthew 25: 31—46 (When did you see me hungry?)

Hand out copies of "Where's Jesus?" (Resource 3A). Let your students work in pairs to complete the sheet. When they're finished, go through the sheet as a group and ask volunteers to share their answers. Use the following information to supplement your students' responses.

Matthew 4:23-25

Describe the people who followed Jesus—were they "first types" or "last types"? (They were suffering from all kinds of sicknesses and diseases—many of which were probably contagious. Some were demon-possessed. It's likely that many of them looked and smelled terrible. In short, they were the kind of people others were probably uncomfortable around.)

(Right before the Sermon on the Mount / the Crowd)

What do you think "normal" people thought of the people Jesus spent His time with? (They probably looked down on those people and wondered why Jesus wasted His time with them.)

What was it about Jesus that appealed to the hurting and lowly people of Jewish society? (The fact that He healed them of their illnesses was probably the major drawing card. But the fact that someone of His stature would spend time with them, caring about their needs, was also probably a big part of it.)

How were the lives of those who followed Jesus changed as a result of His ministry? (Their diseases were cured, allowing them to live a more "normal" life. Beyond that, though, they recognized that they were loved and cared for by the Lord Himself, which probably did wonders for their self-confidence.)

Luke 19:1-9

Describe the person Jesus chose to spend time with in this passage—was he a "first type" or "last type"? (Zacchaeus was a crooked tax collector who was especially hated by the people around him. He became wealthy by overcharging his fellow Jews on their taxes and cheating people out of their money.)

How did the people respond when they saw where Jesus was going? (They did not approve of Jesus choosing to spend His time in Jericho with the town villain. They mumbled and grumbled about Jesus' choice of company.)

How do you suppose Zacchaeus felt? (Zacchaeus probably felt overjoyed by Jesus' visit. He may have also felt unworthy to be in the Lord's presence.)

How did Zacchaeus's life change as a result of the Lord's visit? (He recognized his sin and made up for it by giving back four times the amount he had taken, as well as giving half his possessions to the poor.)

John 4:4-42

Describe the person Jesus chose to spend time with in this passage—was she a "first type" or "last type"? (The Samaritan woman was an unlikely choice for a conversation partner. The first surprise is that she was a Samaritan. The idea of a Jewish person talking civilly with a Samaritan was unheard of at this time. The Jews looked down on the Samaritans and considered them to be second-class citizens. The second surprise is that she was a woman. It was extremely unusual for a religious leader to talk to a woman in such a male-dominated society. Finally, she had been married five times already and was now living with a man who was not her husband—by Jewish standards she was extremely immoral.)

How did the disciples respond when they saw who Jesus was talking to? (The Bible tells us that they were surprised to see Jesus talking to this woman but did not say anything about it.)

How do you suppose the woman felt? (At various points in the conversation she was probably surprised, curious, confused, ashamed, astonished, and grateful.)

What difference do you think Jesus made in the woman's life? (He probably made her feel worthier than she had ever felt. Jesus' talk gave her enough confidence to tell other people in town about Him. She helped convince them that Jesus was the promised Messiah.)

How are Jesus' teachings and example different from what the world tells us? (The world tells us to get ahead at any cost, to step over anyone who gets in our way to the top. Jesus, on the other hand, showed by His example and teachings that we are to head for the bottom of the ladder and to minister to the people we meet there.)

On a scale of one to ten, how hard would you say it is to do what Jesus instructed? How hard would it be for you to stop worrying about getting ahead in your social life and accept the value of being last instead of first? Ask your students to explain their ratings.

Link 3

Predictable Choices

Explain: **Based on the passages we've just studied, what could you do today to follow Jesus' teachings and example about being last in order to be first? *Where* would you spend your time? *How* would you spend your time? *With whom* would you spend your time?**

Hand out copies of "Where Can I Follow Jesus?" (Resource 3B). Let group members work in pairs to complete the sheet. When everyone is finished, ask volunteers to share their ideas as to how they could follow Jesus' example in each of the four locations.

Discuss: **If you want to be a disciple or follower of Jesus, where will you be spending your time—with the "winners" or the "losers"?** (If we want to follow Jesus, we will seek out the people He would go to and treat them with the same respect and care that He would give them. Often those people would be considered the losers by most teens today.)

If you were to make a specific commitment today to valuing the privilege of being last, what would you do? Would you start at home, in your neighborhood, at school, or in your community? How would you change your attitude or actions? Encourage group members to share their ideas.

While students are still paired with their accountability partners, hand out copies of the student journal, "Heart Check: A Practical Approach to Valuing the Least and Last" (Resource 3C). Have each student look at the "Do It Up" section and fill out the plan for what they will do this week to follow Jesus' example of being last and striving to reach out to others. If some accountability pairs finish before others, encourage them to share things that they can pray about for each other during the week.

When you reassemble the group, ask for volunteers to share some of the things they talked about in their pairs. Then take some time to share prayer requests as a large group. Once everyone has had a chance to share, have a time of prayer. Encourage students to pray for the needs that were shared but do not force anyone to pray aloud. Close your prayer time by reminding your students that, in a sense, Jesus was a loser. That's certainly how he appeared on the cross! Yet God exalted Him above all things.

As you conclude the session, point out that the rest of the "Heart Check" student sheet is designed to motivate each group member to set aside a few minutes each day to spend with God. Encourage them to use the sheet as they study God's Word and follow through on their "action plans."

LEARNER LINK

As your students work on the "Do It Up" section of Resource 3C, encourage them to think realistically about how they can put Jesus' teaching into practice. They can begin right at home and at school, which may not seem glamorous, but may actually be more difficult than helping strangers in their larger community.

MAKING IT REAL

A big part of discipleship is encouraging your students to put what they have learned into action. As their leader, you should be constantly looking for teachable moments—times when you are together with the students, outside of your group time, in which you can encourage them to practice what they have been learning. Another great way to do this is to set up service projects or experiential learning times. Session five in this book provides what you need to set up one of these learning experiences.

Where's Jesus?

Find Jesus in the passages below. Read the verses, then answer the questions that follow.

Matthew 4:23-25
Describe the people who followed Jesus—were they "first types" or "last types"?

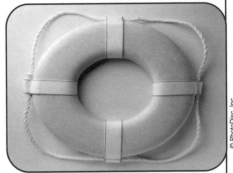

What do you think "normal" people thought of the people Jesus spent His time with?

What was it about Jesus that appealed to the hurting and lowly people of Jewish society?

How were the lives of those who followed Jesus changed as a result of His ministry?

Luke 19:1-9
Describe the person Jesus chose to spend time with in this passage—was he a "first type" or "last type"?

How did the people respond when they saw where Jesus was going?

How do you suppose Zacchaeus felt?

How did Zacchaeus's life change as a result of the Lord's visit?

John 4:4-42
Describe the person Jesus chose to spend time with in this passage—was she a "first type" or "last type"?

How did Jesus' disciples respond when they saw who Jesus was talking to?

How do you suppose the woman felt?

What difference do you think Jesus made in the woman's life?

Where Can I Follow Jesus?

If you were trying to follow Jesus' example of being last in order to be first, how could you do so today in your family, in your neighborhood, in your school, and in your community?

Your Family

Your Neighborhood

Your School

Your Community

HEART CHECK:
A Practical Approach to Valuing the Least and Last

You may think you've picked up some valuable tips for lowering your social standards at today's meeting, but unless you actually put them to use in your life, these tips are worthless. Remember, God wants not only "listeners" of His Word, but "doers" (James 1:22). This sheet is for doers.

LOOK IT UP

Below you'll find seven Scripture references, one for every day of the week. Each passage listed below has something interesting to say about the last being first. Spend a few minutes each day looking up the passage and writing down a few (relevant) thoughts that pop into your head.

DAY ONE: Philippians 2:5-11 (What did Jesus give up for our sakes? How did His Father reward Him for that?)

_____
_____
_____
_____

DAY TWO: Matthew 25:31-46 (Why do you suppose Jesus associated Himself with society's "castoffs"?)

_____
_____
_____
_____

DAY THREE: Mark 2:13-17 (How did Jesus respond to the Pharisees who criticized His choice of dinner companions?)

_____
_____
_____

DAY FOUR: Matthew 5:3-12 (What does this passage tell us about what Jesus considers important in a person?)

_____
_____
_____
_____

☺ TALK IT UP

Jesus assures us that "all things are possible with God" (Mark 10:27). That includes turning our social priority list upside down. So when you're faced with a situation that calls for you to empathize with the "losers," a wise first step is to consult the One who makes all things possible. Take some time to write down a few prayer requests, specific ways in which you need the Lord to help you shift your focus away from yourself. (For example, you might ask Him to help you recognize the needs of others.) Don't be afraid to get personal here. No one else needs to see your prayer request list.

_____
_____
_____
_____
_____
_____
_____
_____
_____
_____
_____
_____
_____
_____
_____
_____
_____
_____
_____
_____

DAY FIVE: Luke 14:12-14 (Why do needy people make such good dinner companions?)

_____

_____

_____

_____

DAY SIX: Luke 18:15-17 (If Jesus wasn't too busy to spend time with children, what should that say to us?)

_____

_____

_____

_____

DAY SEVEN: Matthew 4:23-25 (How comfortable do you think you would have been in the crowd that followed Jesus around? Why?)

_____

_____

_____

_____

DO IT UP

If you're serious about following Jesus' example of considering the needs of others first, you'll need an action plan. Here is one for you to follow:

STEP ONE: Plan!

How will you learn to be content with being least, last, or losing? Put some thought into your response. Don't settle for some lame answer. Be specific. What exactly are you planning to do? When will you do it? How are you going to shift your focus from yourself to others?

STEP TWO: Act

Put your plan into action and then answer these questions. Did it go as you had planned? What did you end up doing? Was it easier or harder than you expected? What kind of response did you get?

STEP THREE: Review!

Do you think you handled these situations in a way Jesus might have handled them? If you had a chance to do it over again, what would you do differently? Do you feel any differently toward the person or people you helped now? Do you think he or she feels any differently about you?

LITTLE BIBLE BACKGROUND

Link 2

Ask your group members to read aloud Matthew 10:39; Matthew 18:2-4; and Mark 9:35. Discuss: **What can we learn about Jesus' nature from these three passages?**
If no one else mentions it, suggest that Jesus viewed life contrary to the way most people view it. He said . . .
• If you want to find your life, you must lose it.
• If you want to achieve Christian maturity, you have to become as a child.
• If you want to be first, you must be last.
Ask: **Do you think we could describe Jesus as a rebel? Why or why not? Do you think we would be considered rebels if we were to live the way He lived? Why or why not?** Encourage debate among students with differing viewpoints.

Link 3

Put this question to your group members: **What is it that can make the thought of hanging around people different from yourself unappealing?** Help your students understand that it's pride and perhaps a little fear that keeps us from reaching out to them. **What makes us think, either consciously or subconsciously, that we are better than other people?** We might dress nicer, our families might have more money, or we haven't gotten into the kind of trouble they have. **Why are we sometimes afraid to hang around with those people?** Often we don't want to be seen with them because we think it will damage our reputation. We don't want our friends to think that we are like them. Briefly discuss some strategies for dealing with pride and fear.

ADVANCED LEARNERS

Link 2

Challenge your advanced students with this question: **When Jesus came to earth, He had a choice of whether to spend most of His time with upper- and middle-class people or with working- and lower-class people. Why do you think He usually chose the second group?** If no one else mentions it, point out that we have done nothing to earn God's favor, and so our natural reaction to the things of God should be humility. That's the attitude the Lord wants from His people. It's an attitude more likely to be found in the underprivileged members of society.

Link 3

Have someone read aloud James 1:22. Discuss: **What's the difference between listening and doing when it comes to making ourselves last as Jesus instructed?** Help your group members see that it's one thing to admit intellectually that all people are valuable to the Lord and that we have a responsibility to those who are underprivileged. It's quite another thing to "get our hands dirty" by actually helping someone in need.

MOSTLY GUYS

Link 1

Rather than using the "Hot Potato" game with your group of guys, try an endurance test. Ask your group members to stand up, lift one leg off the ground, and balance themselves for as long as they can. When any body part except the bottom of one foot touches the ground, a person is out. Continue the contest until only one person remains. Introduce the topic of the session with this question: **Can you think of any other areas of life in which the last person finishes first?** See if anyone mentions the Christian life.

Link 2

Here's a just-for-fun question for your guys to answer: **How you would explain Jesus' strategy of being last to a win-at-all-costs athletic coach?** Ask some of your guys to demonstrate how they think their coaches would respond if they were asked to apply Jesus' principle in a football, basketball, or baseball game.

MOSTLY GIRLS

Link 2

Replace the story of Zaccheus on Resource 3A with the story of the sinful woman in Luke 7:36-50. Use these questions to guide your discussion:
- **Describe the person Jesus chose to spend time with in this passage.**
- **How did the people respond when they saw what was happening?**
- **How do you suppose the woman felt?**
- **How do you suppose the woman's life changed as a result of her encounter with the Lord?**

Link 3

Give your girls something to think about with this question: **Where does safety fit into the equation? If we're going to spend time with the underprivileged, the homeless, and the needy, we're going to put ourselves in some places and some situations we've never faced before. What can we do to make sure that we're safe?** First of all, your girls can start associating with the "undesirable" right at school, helping the needy in a relatively safe environment. As for other situations, your girls may suggest prayer, which is a great start, but they should also consider some preventative strategies like never traveling alone and never going to unsafe neighborhoods after dark. If they want to be involved in service projects, they should go with organized groups and always be sure somebody knows where they are and when they expect to be back.

MEDIA

Link 1

Needed: Video clip: *The Man in the Iron Mask, All of Me, Trading Places, 18 Again! Like Father, Like Son, etc.*

Show some clips from *The Man in the Iron Mask, All of Me, Trading Places, 18 Again! Like Father, Like Son*, or any other movie whose plot involves switching identities. Watch a few scenes (which you've screened beforehand for suitability) in which the characters have trouble adjusting to their new identities.

Discuss: **How hard would it be for you to switch identities with someone from a much more difficult background than you've experienced—say, someone who's homeless or unemployed? How hard would it be for you to drop to the bottom of the social ladder in our society?** Get a few responses.

Explain: **You may never have to actually *live* that way, but Jesus wants you to experience people who do.** Move on to the Bible study in Link 2.

Link 3
Needed: Newspaper

Bring in a newspaper with a community calendar section in it. Find some activities designed to benefit the underprivileged in your community that your students can participate in as their first step toward serving those who are in need.

EXTRA ADRENALINE
Link 1
Needed: Plate of goodies with a sign on it

Just as your students get settled in their chairs for the meeting, announce that there's a plate full of goodies waiting for them in a room on the other side of the building or out on the front lawn. Then add: **The last one there is out of luck.** This should send your group members on a mad scramble for the snacks. When they get to the plate, however, they will discover a sign on top of the goodies that reads, "Reserved for the person who's out of luck." Give the plate to the last person who arrives. When you get back to the room, explain: **This is an example of the discipleship truth we're going to talk about today: If you want to be first, you have to be last. Let's see how that applies in areas other than refreshments.**

Link 2
Needed: Two serving trays and several plastic or paper cups

Introduce the idea of servanthood (putting the needs of others ahead of our own) with an activity called "Servant's Relay." Divide your group into two teams. Have students line up in classic relay-race fashion. Give the first person in each line a serving tray with several tall, skinny plastic or paper cups on it. Team members will race to the far wall and back, balancing the tray in one hand. At no time may a contestant touch the tray with two hands. If a cup falls off the tray, the person must stop to pick it up before continuing on. Declare the members of the winning team to be champion potential servants.

JUNIOR HIGH
Link 1
Have your students pair up for a race. One person will stand behind the other with his hands holding the back of the shirt or the belt loop of his partner. The pairs will run forward to the far wall, without breaking contact, and then backward all the way back, so that the last person in the pair finishes first. After you've run a few heats, ask: **Can you think of any other areas of life in which the *last* person finishes first?** If no one else mentions them suggest that endurance contests and the Christian life both fit the description.

Link 2
Ask: **Have you ever been snubbed or made fun of by someone because of the way you looked, the place you come from, the way you talk, or anything else you can't help about yourself?** If so, how did

it make you feel? Explain that this is just a taste of what some people go through every day. These are the people Jesus instructs us to serve.

Planning Checklist

LINK 1: The Joy of Being Last
❑ Mostly Guys
❑ Media
❑ Extra Adrenaline
❑ Junior High

LINK 2: Do What?
❑ Little Bible Background
❑ Advanced Learners
❑ Mostly Guys
❑ Mostly Girls
❑ Extra Adrenaline
❑ Junior High

LINK 3: Predictable Choices
❑ Little Bible Background
❑ Advanced Learners
❑ Mostly Girls
❑ Media

LET'S GO RACING
(Perseverance)

Key Questions
- What is perseverance?
- What example did Jesus set in persevering despite the obstacles He faced?
- How can you persevere and be successful in the race that has been marked for you?

Bible Base
Matthew 4:1-11
Matthew 12:1-14
Matthew 26:36-45, 47-50
Matthew 27:45-46
Luke 22:54-62; Hebrews 12:1-3

Supplies
- Bibles
- Pencils
- Copies of Resources 4A, 4B, Journal

Opener (Optional)

Easy, Once You Know How

Are you an accomplished juggler? If not, recruit someone you know who is. Bring this person to your meeting and let him or her try to teach your students how to juggle in five minutes. Encourage your instructor to emphasize the patience and perseverance it takes to learn juggling. When he or she is finished speaking, give your students a chance to try their hand at it. They will soon discover the meaning of patience and perseverance as their juggling balls go flying all over the place.

LEARNER LINK

Many of the students in your group have definite self-images by this age in their lives. At this age, they have already formed opinions about what they think they are good at, and what they think they are not. As a result, some of your students will try to avoid activities in which they believe they might fail. Encourage your students to not just persevere, but first, risk and try something, regardless of how they think they might do.

Introduce the session topic this way: **If you want to learn to juggle well, you have to be able to persevere through the frustration and difficulties. The same is true with the Christian life. If you want succeed as a Christian, you will have to persevere through many frustrations and difficult times.**

Link 1

MAKING IT REAL

One of the benefits of leading a small discipleship group is the chance to reach out to some of the parents and families of the students. Make a point, any chance you get, to talk with them and to let them know what you have been doing in your group. Parents appreciate that and it can help them encourage their students at home. Not all of the parents may be Christians so be aware that they are looking for the characteristics of Jesus in your life.

If There Was One Thing I Could Change . . .

If you handed out Resource 3C at the end of Session 3, take a few minutes to find out how your students' planned attempts at "being last" went. Ask volunteers to share their experiences with the rest of the group.

Hand out copies of "Top Ten Complaints of the First Disciples" (Resource 4A). Give group members a minute or two to look over the list.

Discuss: **If we were to make a list of the top ten *modern* disciple complaints, what kinds of things would be on it?** Encourage your students to let loose here about the things that bother them about Christianity, the Bible, misconceptions about their faith, or any other element of Christianity. Give them the freedom to suggest humorous responses as well as serious ones.

What are some of the *good* things about being a disciple? What is it that keeps you going day-in and day-out? It should be interesting to hear what your group members have to say on this topic. After you've received a few responses, explain: **Today we're going to be talking about the importance of perseverance in a disciple's life.**

Link 2

The Race Is On

We've talked about some of the things that disciples have had to endure. What are some things that Jesus had to endure during His time here on earth?

6 Scriptures

Have your students work in pairs and assign each pair one or two of the following passages. Students should read their assigned verses and decide what Jesus had to endure in that passage. The Scriptures are: Matthew 4:1-11; Matthew 12:1-14; Matthew 26:36-45; Matthew 26:47-50; Matthew 27:45-46; and Luke 22:54-62. After a few minutes have students share their answers.

- Matthew 4:1-11: Jesus endured temptation by Satan.

- Matthew 12:1-14: Jesus endured all kinds of disbelief and accusations from the religious leaders of the day.

- Matthew 26:36-45: Jesus endured the pain in Gethsemane without even a friend to stay awake with Him.

- Matthew 26:47-50: Jesus endured betrayal by one of His own disciples and arrest.

- Matthew 27:45-46: Jesus endured separation from God the Father at His death.

- Luke 22:54-62: Jesus endured the denial of one of His best friends.

Spend a few minutes discussing how each of these things Jesus endured must have felt. How would your students feel if they had to endure something similar?

Do you think that Jesus ever felt like just giving up? Encourage your students to share their opinions honestly, and to back them up with Scripture if possible.

Why was it important for Jesus not to give up? Why did He have to persevere in order to succeed? Jesus came to earth to fulfill a very specific task. In order to restore relationship between God and humanity and bring His followers eternal life, Jesus had to persevere. If He didn't keep going and endure the pain of crucifixion and separation from God, our salvation would not have been possible.

What kept Him going? Jesus kept going because He was determined to carry out the will of His Father who sent Him. He spent plenty of time with His Father in prayer, and He knew the Scriptures so well that He could refute the religious leaders and even Satan with His use of Scripture. Jesus also had a small group of close friends who frequently let Him down but probably also offered some support.

How can we persevere like Jesus did? We can use the same tools Jesus used: prayer and time in God's Word. We can also have a small group of friends to support us.

[handwritten: Which is easier to do/focus on cross? ① or look ② sideways?]

Link 3

[handwritten: John 21: 15-22 (Jesus restores Peter)]

Obstacle Removal

The apostle Paul also offered some suggestions as to how we can persevere by following Jesus' example. Let's take a look.

[handwritten: but Peter looks sideways]

Have someone read Hebrews 12:1-3. Discuss: **What is this race and who marked it out for us?** Explain that the race is each believer's life, complete with all the troubles to be endured and all the obstacles to be overcome. Point out that the Lord has set up individual courses for every one of His followers. None of us runs on the exact same course.

[handwritten: Focus on the Cross]

Why is it so important to keep our eyes on Jesus while we run? (We keep our eyes on Jesus in order to follow His example. He knows how to run the race better than anyone. We can learn from His endurance and perseverance. Also, if we are focused on Him, we won't be so easily distracted or fall over the obstacles.)

[handwritten: Do not look right and left! Why?]

What is perseverance? Why is it important for us to persevere? (Perseverance is the determination to continue regardless of the obstacles we face or the difficulty of the task. It's important because the race that lies before us is long, difficult, and full of obstacles. We're going to stumble and fall. We'll get tired. We'll feel like quitting. If we have perseverance, though, we will get back up, get our second wind, and continue. Only if we persevere can we succeed in the race that God has given us to run.)

Refer back to Hebrews 12:1. Ask: **What are some things that hinder us and some sins that entangle?** Get a few responses before moving on. Hand out copies of "Everything that Hinders" (Resource 4B). Let students work in pairs to complete the sheet. Divide the obstacles on the sheet as evenly as possible among the pairs.

Have the pairs answer two questions for each item on the sheet: **How might this be an obstacle or a hindrance on a believer's road to spiritual success?** and **How can you follow Jesus' example to endure or overcome this obstacle on your road to spiritual success?** Give the pairs a few minutes to work. When they're finished, go through the sheet one item at a time, asking pairs to share their responses. Use the following information to supplement their answers. *[handwritten: (What to do!)]*

Busy Schedule
If you're a morning person, set your alarm 15-20 minutes earlier than normal and use that time to talk with God and study His Word. If you're a night person, take 15-20 minutes before you go to bed as your quiet time. Take a look at your activities and prioritize them so that you leave room for time with God.

Doubt
Things happen that will cause you to question your beliefs. Rather than being hindered by your doubts, you should learn to address them head-on. God isn't threatened or angered by your doubts; in fact, He wants you to take them straight to Him! If you really want answers to your questions, ask God and His Holy Spirit will direct you to the places you need to look. Learn to ask and then learn to listen.

Fear of failure is, my biggest fear... what's yours?

Frustration

Noticing a change in your spiritual maturity can be like trying to lose weight. At first you don't see any results. If you persevere, as Jesus did in teaching His disciples, you will eventually see results.

Parents

Not all parents are supportive of their teens' spiritual growth. Remain committed and consistent in your Christian walk and let your life be a witness to them. Don't bash them over the head with your beliefs, but be willing to talk with them when appropriate or when they ask you to.

Popularity

Standing up for your beliefs can be tough. But if you base your selfworth on your relationship with the Lord instead of on what others think of you, you can see yourself in the best possible light.

Fear of Embarrassment

If you're the type of person who's uncomfortable with confrontation or who's shy about speaking up, there's a good chance that you may embarrass yourself in front of other people. This is a case of practice making perfect. The more you talk openly about your faith, the more comfortable you'll become—and the less embarrassment you'll feel.

Friends

In an effort to maintain friendships, some people "water down" their beliefs and scale back their commitment level. But remember, you may be the closest thing to Jesus that your friends ever meet, so don't miss the opportunity to witness to them with your life as well as your words.

Temptation

Jesus used God's Word to resist temptation, and we can do the same. You will not be able to resist temptation on your own. You need God's help, so get in the habit now of talking with Him.

LEARNER LINK

If you're looking for openness and vulnerability from your group members in their responses to these questions, you should be prepared to model such behavior yourself. Share some of your own experiences when you felt like giving up. Talk frankly about how you dealt with those situations. It is great if you can be a good example to your groups, but don't give them the impression that you are beyond such struggles. Don't be afraid to talk about less-than-flattering aspects of your personality. You won't lose the respect of your group members for being honest. In fact, you may be surprised at how much respect you gain. Everyone appreciates a person who isn't afraid to tell the truth.

MAKING IT R E A L

Don't give your students the impression that it's always easy to follow Jesus' example! If you don't acknowledge the challenges, some of your group members may leave with unrealistic expectations. Prepare your students for these unfortunate possibilities by talking honestly about how people may respond to them and risks that are involved in being a disciple of Jesus Christ. Rather than discouraging your group members, you may find that your straightforward approach actually motivates many of them.

Before you wrap up today's session, have your students pair up with their accountability partners. (If you didn't assign accountability partners in Session 1, let students stay in the pairs they were in.) Ask the partners to talk briefly about the obstacle in their life that's giving them the most problems lately. If you think they would be comfortable with it, ask the partners to pray together about those obstacles.

Hand out copies of "Heart Check: A Practical Approach to Perseverance" (Resource 4C). Have students look at the "Do It Up" section and fill out their plan for getting past obstacles this week. If some accountability pairs finish before others, encourage them to share things that they can pray about for each other during the week.

As you conclude the session, point out that the rest of the "Heart Check" student sheet is designed to motivate each group member to set aside a few minutes each day to spend with God. Encourage them to use the sheet as they study God's Word and follow through on their "action plans."

Top Ten Complaints of the First Disciples

10. When you hang out with the Messiah, you always have to be on your best behavior.

9. Some of the fishermen in the group aren't exactly "fresh as daisies," if you know what we mean.

8. The Lord refuses to use schedules and itineraries. We never know whether we're heading for Samaria or the Sea of Galilee.

7. The Pharisees are always trying to make us look bad.

6. It's hard to find peace and quiet with crowds around all the time.

5. Sometimes it's hard to understand a guy who talks in parables.

4. Everywhere we go, it's walk, walk, walk. Our feet are killing us!

3. We can never call in sick, because Jesus will just heal us.

2. None of us is exactly sure how all of this is going to end.

1. Every dumb thing we say and do is being recorded in the Bible.

Everything that Hinders

Some of these may not be obstacles to everyone, but each of them is a hurdle to someone. Write in some of the ways you can overcome each of these obstacles.

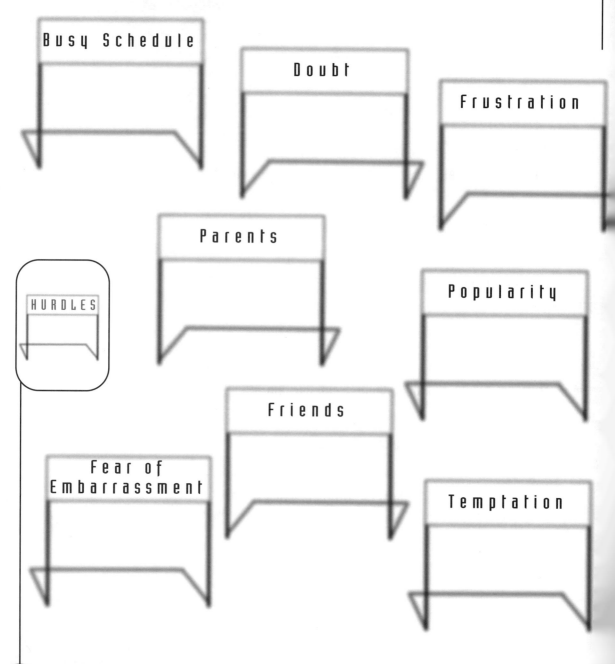

Busy Schedule

Doubt

Frustration

HURDLES

Parents

Popularity

Friends

Fear of Embarrassment

Temptation

HEART CHECK:
A Practical Approach to Perseverance

You may think you've picked up some valuable tips for "running the race" at today's meeting, but unless you actually put them to use in your life, these tips are worthless. Remember, God wants not only "listeners" of His Word, but "doers" (James 1:22). This sheet is for doers.

LOOK IT UP

Below you'll find seven Scripture references, one for every day of the week. Each passage listed below has something interesting to say about persevering in the Christian life. Spend a few minutes each day looking up the passage and jotting down a few (relevant) ideas that pop into your head while you're thinking about it.

DAY ONE: James 1:12 (What is the crown of life that awaits those who persevere?)_____
_____
_____
_____
_____

DAY TWO: Romans 5:3-4 (What kind of suffering has produced perseverance in your life?)_____
_____
_____
_____
_____

DAY THREE: 1 Corinthians 13:4-7 (What role does perseverance play in human love?)_____
_____
_____
_____
_____

DAY FOUR: Hebrews 11:24-29 (Why did Moses persevere?)_____
_____
_____
_____
_____

☺ TALK IT UP

Jesus assures us that "all things are possible with God" (Mark 10:27). That includes persevering on our way to spiritual growth and success. So when we're faced with a really difficult situation, like resisting temptation, a wise first step is to consult the One who makes all things possible. Take some time to write down a few prayer requests, specific ways in which you need the Lord to help you persevere. (For example, you might ask Him to help you get rid of the anger that causes trouble for you.) Don't be afraid to get personal here. No one else needs to see your prayer request list.

_____
_____
_____
_____
_____
_____
_____
_____
_____
_____
_____
_____
_____
_____
_____
_____
_____
_____

DAY FIVE: James 1:2-4 (How and why is our faith tested?)

_____
_____
_____
_____
_____

DAY SIX: 2 Thessalonians 1:4 (How can other people recognize perseverance in you?)

_____
_____
_____
_____

DAY SEVEN: Revelation 2:1-3 (What keeps some people from growing weary when they encounter hardship because of their faith?)

_____
_____
_____
_____

DO IT UP

If you're serious about running the race the Lord has marked out for you, you'll need a plan of action. Here is one to follow:

STEP ONE: **Plan!**

What are you going to do this week to overcome an obstacle in your life? Put some thought into your response. Don't settle for some lame answer. Be specific. What exactly are you planning to do? When will you do it? How are you going to deal with the fallout of your actions?

STEP TWO: **Act!**

Put your plan into action and then answer these questions. Did it go as you planned? What did you end up doing? Was it easier or harder than you expected? What kind of response did you get, if any?

STEP THREE: **Review!**

Do you think you've improved your chances for finishing the race that's marked out for you? Knowing what you know now, would you do anything differently? If so, what and why?

Lesson #5 (use this and other unused items from Lessons 1-4)

LITTLE BIBLE BACKGROUND

Link 2

Take a minute or two to acquaint your Bible "rookies" with one or two members of the great cloud of witnesses named in Hebrews 11 who set examples of faithfulness for us to follow. For instance, if you choose Moses as an example, you might explain to your group members his life story (from Hebrew baby to Pharaoh's son to leader of the Exodus to one who had close fellowship with God) and the work he accomplished (leading the children of Israel out of Egypt and right up to the Promised Land).

Link 3

Help your students understand the "perseverance chain." Ask someone to read Romans 5:3-5 aloud. Discuss the passage using the following questions: What kind of suffering produces perseverance? What is "character" and what does it have to do with perseverance? How does character produce hope? Ultimately, what are the benefits of perseverance? How does this relate to success in the race that God has planned for us?

ADVANCED LEARNERS

Link 2

Go through the list of faith heroes in Hebrews 11, the ones who make up the great cloud of witnesses a chapter later, asking your group members to call out what we can learn from each person's story. Don't take too much time with this activity. Just call out a name and then let your students call out a response. For example, if you were to say, Abraham, one of your students may reply, "Nothing is impossible for God."

Link 3

Add one more obstacle to Resource 4B: *cockiness*. Use the following information to supplement your group members' responses.

It's easy to feel like you've heard it all before if you grew up in the church and have been exposed to God's Word your entire life. It's easy to confuse Bible knowledge with spiritual maturity. It's easy to confuse church attendance with discipleship.

The good news is that cockiness is quite often a phase. In time, and with some effort on your part, you will begin to see your true spiritual condition. You may not like what you see, but you will see it.

MOSTLY GUYS

Link 1

Needed: Several obstacles

Replace the "Top Ten Complaints of the First Disciples" (Resource 4A) activity with a physical challenge for your guys. Have everyone stand up. Place some kind of obstacle next to half of your guys. You might use a small trash can, a stool, two shoe boxes stacked on top of each other, or anything else that is no taller than knee-high as an obstacle. Explain that when you say, **Go,** everyone will start running in place. When you say **Jump,** the guys who are standing next to obstacles must jump over them and continue running. Say **Jump**, every five seconds or so. If you have to, keep your guys running for three minutes or more, until all but the most fit are exhausted. If all goes according to plan, the guys who jumped back and forth over the obstacles will wear out—and perhaps quit—before the other runners.

Afterward, discuss: **Why did such a little obstacle make such a big difference in how long you ran?** After you get a few responses, explain: **Today we're going to be talking about how obstacles can affect the way we "run" as disciples.**

Link 3

Put these questions to your guys: **Do you believe in the old saying, "No pain, no gain"? If so, give me some examples of times when pain led to gain in your life.** If you've got some athletes in the group, you'll probably hear stories of how weightlifting improved their physiques. If you've got gearheads, skateboarders, or in-line skaters in the group, you'll probably hear how the pains of falling eventually gave way to the satisfaction of learning a new trick.

Discuss: **Do you believe pain is necessary in order to see gains in the Christian life? Should our spiritual muscles be aching as we run the race of the Christian life? Explain your answer.**

MOSTLY GIRLS

Link 2

Refer your girls to Hebrews 11:31, which mentions Rahab, the only woman listed by name among the heroes of the faith. You might even direct your girls back to Joshua 2:1-21, which describes Rahab's faithful act of hiding the Israelite spies even though they were supposed to be her enemies. Ask: **Who are some other heroines of the faith that are cheering you on while you're running the race?** Encourage your girls to talk about the women of the Bible whose examples they most admire.

Link 3

Focus your discussion on the "Friends" obstacle. Get your girls' responses to these questions: **How important are your friends in your life? What roles do your friends play? How do you think your closest friends would react if you were to be a little more "obvious" about your discipleship? How much of an impact do you think their response would have on you? Would you consider your friends to be an obstacle in your Christian life? Why or why not?**

MEDIA

Link 2

Needed: Video clip: pregame show

Before the session, you'll need to record the beginning of a televised sporting event. What you want is a snippet of a sportscaster "setting the scene" for the game (or race or contest). Usually these pregame comments include a description of the crowd in attendance, a recap of the competitors' records or standings, and maybe a special-interest profile of one of the competitors. Play the scene for your group members. Then ask two volunteers to do a similar pregame summary for the race described in Hebrews 12:1-3. These sportscasters might describe the cloud of witnesses at the race, give some background on the imaginary runner, and describe the condition of the race course.

Link 3

Needed: Video clip: Game show

After you've taped a sports pregame show (see Link 1), record a game show in which people go to extreme lengths—even to the point of embarrassment—in order to win prizes. If your cable system carries the Game Show Network, record clips of the old Gong Show, in which contestants made fools of themselves in order to win a meager check. Nickelodeon also carries some goofy game shows that you can use. Show the clip to your group members.

Discuss: **Why do you think these people were willing to go to such extremes for a simple contest? How far would you be willing to go to improve your chances in the race that has been marked for you?**

EXTRA ADRENALINE

Link 1

Needed: Obstacles for obstacle course, stopwatch

Set up an obstacle course in your room, using chairs (to run around), tables (to crawl under), curtain rods (to jump up and touch), and anything else you can find. Use a stopwatch to time each competitor. Depending on the size of your group, let each person run the course two or three times. If you want to make things really official, post the contestants' best times. After you've declared a winner, introduce the session topic this way: **Sometimes the Christian life is like an obstacle course. The difference is, in real life the obstacles are harder to get around. We're going to be talking about those obstacles today.**

Link 3

Have your students race across the room again as in Link 1, only this time with no obstacles. This time your students will be running "unhindered" to one side of the room and back. Use your stopwatch to see how much their times improve without the obstacles. After you've declared a winner, wrap up the activity with this question: **How would removing obstacles from your Christian life make things easier for you?**

JUNIOR HIGH

Opener

Kick things off with a talent show. Give each of your group members a minute or so to demonstrate his or her talent. Your students' talents may include anything from kazoo playing to juggling to rapping. (You may want to make arrangements for this ahead of time by asking your group members to bring in musical instruments or anything else they need for their performance. Advance warning will also give your students time to practice and prepare.)

When everyone is finished, discuss: **How long did it take you to learn the skill you just showed us? Were there times when you felt like giving up or quitting? If so, what made you hang in there?**

Introduce the session this way: **Today we're going to be talking about what makes us "hang in there" when we feel like giving up as disciples of Jesus.**

Link 3

Replace one of the obstacles on Resource 4B (perhaps "Frustration") with "Confusion." Use the following information to supplement your group members' responses.

Many young people believe that Christian responsibilities are for older people and not them. They claim the Bible is too hard to understand and that it's written for adults, not teenagers. They convince themselves that they're off the hook as far as Christian responsibilities go until they get "old enough" to study God's Word. Their confusion causes them to miss out on spiritual growth that they could be enjoying.

The longer you stick with Bible study—regardless of how hard it may seem—the better you will get at understanding God's Word. There are some things you can do to make Bible study easier for yourself, things like using easy-to-understand versions of the Bible, study Bibles created especially for young people, and finding mature believers to talk to when you have questions.

Planning Checklist

OPENER: Easy, Once You Know How
❏ Junior High

LINK 1: If There Was One Thing I Could Change . . .
❏ Mostly Guys
❏ Extra Adrenaline

LINK 2: The Race Is On
❏ Little Bible Background
❏ Advanced Learners
❏ Mostly Girls
❏ Media

LINK 3: Obstacle Removal
❏ Little Bible Background
❏ Advanced Learners
❏ Mostly Guys
❏ Mostly Girls
❏ Media
❏ Extra Adrenaline
❏ Junior High

REALITY CHECK: STRIVING TOGETHER

About This Session

This bonus session is designed to help your group members understand discipleship in a deeper, more hands-on way. The four sessions of this book cover what it means to measure success as Jesus did. True discipleship involves the heart, the head, and the hands. During this session you'll give your students a chance to take the things that they are learning and experiencing and put them into practice in the real world. This experiential learning time is a good way to wrap up your four weeks of study, but it can also be done at any point throughout the study.

Check It Out

You'll need to do some advance preparation for this activity—and perhaps plan for significant travel time (or an overnight stay). Explain to your students that just discussing and studying about Jesus' standards of success is incomplete. To be truly successful as Jesus wants, we will take His words and put them into action by helping others. Here are some ideas to help your students do just that.

Contact a local or regional camping facility that has a "ropes course." YMCA camps often have such courses—a series of wall-and-log obstacles and rope-climbing challenges that require a spirit of intense cooperation and teamwork. In order for any one person to be successful, all must pull together and extend a helping hand. This is a fantastic team-building activity for any group. And it will lend itself well to reinforcing the message of measuring success as Jesus did.

If going to such a camp is not an option for your group, you can plan your own time of team-building activities in a local park. Consult your local library for activity ideas, or use some of these.

2x4 Challenge:
Place a narrow board at least 10 or 12 feet long on the ground. Have your students form two teams, one at either end of the board. Everyone must stand on the board and, without touching the ground, the two teams must cross to the opposite ends of the board.

Cooperative Creativity:
Have your students form groups of three. In each group, one person must not speak, one person must keep his or her eyes closed, and one person must wear earplugs. Give each group a piece of paper and challenge them to make a drinking container from it.

Spatially Challenged:
Mark off three squares on the ground, one approximately 4'x4', the next 3'x3', and the last 2'x2'. Have students work together to fit everyone into the largest square without any body part touching the ground outside of the square. Once they've met that challenge, have them fit into the middle-size square, and finally the smallest square, without any body part touching the ground outside of the square.

Joined at the Hip:
Take your students on a hike. The twist to this hike is that all your students will be joined together by a rope around the waist. Whenever one person needs to rest, everyone must rest. Every student must help everyone else to succeed.

Take It Deeper

Go a little deeper by helping your students get involved with special needs students. What could they do to help these youth succeed in some way? Spend time discussing what success would look like in this kind of outreach project, and then get busy planning the event! Perhaps your students would spend a morning or afternoon at a facility for handicapped children. They could get involved in the physical care-taking chores. Again, you might want to contact your local YMCA or Red Cross to see if they offer any opportunities to spend time with special needs students.

As another option, your group could plan a party or sporting event for those with special needs. You may want to look at the team-building ideas from the previous page to see if any can be adapted and used at your party or event. Be sure the idea springs from your group in order to maintain students' sense of ownership. Stress the concept of Jesus' definition of success and the example of Jesus in coming to help the "needy" (which includes all of us!).

Think It Through

Ideally you will spend most of your debriefing time listening to your group members' experiences in the "real world." Encourage your students to share their feelings about Jesus' definition of success. If you need some discussion guides, use any or all of the following questions.

• **What have you learned about how Jesus measured success? How have you changed as a result?**

• **How were you able to make a difference in the lives of others?**

• **What, specifically, can we do to become spiritually successful or to make our lights shine more brightly for those around us to see?**

• **Let's say years from now you are asked by a group of young Christians to speak about what it means to be successful in life. What advice would you give them?**

Close the meeting with a word of prayer. Thank God for your group members and their willingness to commit themselves to discipleship, despite the hard work and selflessness that it requires. Ask God to help your students continue to seek success on His terms.

Name	Address	Phone	Parent Names	e-mail	B-day	Notes
1.						
2.						
3.						
4.						
5.						
6.						
7.						
8.						
9.						
10.						
11.						
12.						
13.						
14.						
15.						

Lift IT UP

Ephesians 3:16 "I pray that out of his glorious riches he may strengthen you with power through his Spirit in your inner being, so that Christ may dwell in your hearts through faith. And I pray that you, being rooted and established in love, may have power, together with all the saints to grasp how wide and long and high and deep is the love of Christ, and to know this love that surpasses knowledge—that you may be filled to the measure of all the fullness of God."

_____   _____
_____   _____
_____   _____
_____   _____
_____   _____
_____   _____
_____   _____
_____   _____
_____   _____
_____   _____
_____   _____
_____   _____
_____   _____
_____   _____
_____   _____
_____   _____
_____   _____
_____   _____
_____   _____
_____   _____
_____   _____
_____   _____

Jonathan London

THE LION
WHO HAD ASTHMA

Pictures by **Nadine Bernard Westcott**

ALBERT WHITMAN & COMPANY
MORTON GROVE, ILLINOIS

For my son Sean
and every child who has ever had asthma,
and for my wife, Maureen Weisenberger,
the lion's mother, with love.
With thanks to
Paula Pearce, Director of Programs,
American Lung Association of the Redwood Empire,
and for Sean's pediatrician, Jeffrey Miller, M.D. *J.L.*

For Becky and Wendy. *N.B.W.*

A NOTE FOR PARENTS
OF CHILDREN WHO HAVE ASTHMA

When our son, the Sean (pronounced Shawn) of this story, had his first asthma attack as a baby, we had to rush him to an emergency room in the middle of the night. It was a distressing experience for all of us.

We soon learned much about asthma, a lung disease which causes breathing problems for almost ten million Americans. Around three million are children under the age of eighteen. It is the most common chronic disease of childhood.

There is no cure for asthma yet, but the symptoms, such as coughing and wheezing, can be controlled. And attacks, or "episodes," can be stopped once they have begun. There are various treatments for asthma, and they are aimed at preventing as well as stopping episodes.

Now four years old, Sean has his own nebulizer for use at home, and the experience is far more manageable. The nebulizer turns liquid medicine into a mist which is easy for him to inhale through a mask. Sean's nebulizer is the machine shown in this book; there are also several other types of nebulizers.

Sean's medicine, administered with the nebulizer, is a bronchodilator. It relaxes the muscles in the airway walls and helps open the airways.

Relaxes is a key word; relaxing makes being sick easier to bear and to control. Breathing exercises and visualization help lead to relaxation. Visualization is a product of the imagination, and like most young children, Sean has a great imagination. Encourage a child's imagination! It is not only an asset in the treatment of asthma but enhances life itself.

Jonathan London

Sean is a lion
roaring in the jungle.

Now he's a hippo
singing in the bathtub.

At suppertime,
he's a **G I A N T**
munching trees . . .
C-a-a-*runch!*

Now he's a lion again,
with awesome teeth
and fearsome claws.
Grrrrrrrrrroww . . .

Cough, cough—

The lion has a cough.
His chest hurts,
and it's hard for him
to breathe.

The lion has asthma.

Instead of growling and roaring, he wheezes.
It sounds like there's a squeaky whistle
inside him when he breathes.

The lion feels tired
and a little bit frightened.
He feels like crying.

"It's time for your treatment,
Sean," says his mom.

Sean doesn't feel like being a lion anymore.
He curls up and cries
and coughs and coughs
and breathes faster and faster.

"Okay, Sean," says his mom.
"Quiet, now. Just breathe soft and easy.
Here's your mask. Time to be a pilot!"

Sean sits up and puts on his mask.
He says, "*I* want to turn it on!"

He presses the power switch,
and the machine starts up.
It's noisy, like a jet taking off.

In his mask,
Sean is a jet pilot
flying high in the sky.

The steam is the clouds.
The knobs are the controls.
Zoooooom! he goes, Jet Pilot Sean,
flying faster and faster,
higher and higher.

"Breathe deep, Jet Pilot Sean,"
says his dad,
with arms spread like wings.

Sean's chest doesn't hurt now.
His coughing has stopped,
and the wheezing sound, too.
He can *breathe!*

Sean stops flying
and comes down for a landing.

He's a lion again—
the King of the Jungle.

The illustrations are watercolor and ink.
The text typeface is Bookman Regular.

Library of Congress Cataloging-in-Publication Data

London, Jonathan, 1947—
The lion who had asthma / Jonathan London;
illustrated by Nadine Bernard Westcott.
p. c.m.
Summary: Sean's nebulizer mask and his imagination aid in his recovery following an asthma attack. Includes information on childhood asthma and how to control its symptoms.
ISBN 0-8075-4559-7 (hardcover)
ISBN 0-8075-4560-0 (paperback)
[1. Asthma—Fiction. 2. Imagination—Fiction.]
I. Westcott, Nadine Bernard, ill. II. Title.
PZ7.L8432Li 1992   91-16553
[E]—dc20   CIP
                                                      AC

ABOUT THE AUTHOR

Jonathan London's poetry and short stories have appeared in over one hundred magazines. This is his second book for children. Jonathan lives in Graton, California, with his wife, Maureen, and their sons, Sean and Aaron. He has traveled all over the world and, when not writing, loves to kayak, hike, dance, and read. He has held a variety of jobs, among them dancer, cannery worker, laborer, landscaper, bookstore clerk, counselor at a juvenile home, display installer at trade shows, and poet in the schools.

ABOUT THE ARTIST

Nadine Bernard Westcott began her art career as a greeting card designer for Hallmark Cards in Kansas City. After moving to Vermont, she married her husband, Bill, and in 1980 they founded their own greeting card company, Hartland Cards. Her work creating humorous cards led Nadine to publish her first children's book in 1980. Since then, she has written and illustrated or illustrated more than fifteen books for children, among them *Even Little Kids Get Diabetes*.

Nadine lives in Woodstock, Vermont, with her husband and their daughters, Becky and Wendy. The family spends summers on the island of Nantucket.